MW01145551

A
Journey
of Hope

For Parents of Struggling Children

Anna R. Buck

Published by
Anna's House LLC,
Northglenn, Colorado

The stories in this book are true, although the names have been changed.

A Journey of Hope
For Parents of Struggling Children

Copyright © 2014 by Anna R. Buck

First edition:
ISBN 978-0-9814796-8-2

Library of Congress Control Number:
2015902204

Published by Anna's House, LLC
Northglenn, Colorado
www.AnnasHouseLLC.com

Editor: Kristin Wright-Bettner
Cover Design: Barbara J. Foos
Cover images: Courtesy of Pixabay
Chapter One Photos: Courtesy of Jimmy and Melissa Stewart
Printed in Canada by Friesens

"A Journey of Hope is a brilliant account of one success story after another! As a licensed Montessori teacher who can deeply appreciate individualized programs for children, I have observed that Anna's courageous work meets each child at the origin of their own unique struggles. Over the years, I've pointed numerous colleagues and families toward Anna's system of forward thinking therapy. This book is a must read, for both parents and educators alike."

Carrie M. Sarazin, Licensed Montessori Upper
El teacher, Licensed teacher with state CO; Golden, CO

"A Journey of Hope is of profound importance to our understanding of child development and education. Anna's approach to Neuro-Developmental Delay is effective and easily done with commitment and consistency. It is based on sound scientific principles of the nervous system and how it develops. This program has my enthusiastic support as I have personally seen the benefits with my eight-year-old son."

Bridgett Burling, PT, Rapid City, SD

"As a doctor of chiropractic and a father of a son with NDD, we tried many different therapies and NDD therapy is the only one that has worked for our son. NDD therapy has been a breath of fresh air.

This book gives the answers to many of the unanswered problems that children are suffering with today, getting to the cause of the problem instead of treating the symptoms or masking them. If this were the standard first line of treatment, it would change our world and save our children from being misdiagnosed and mistreated."

Dr. Jon Wall DC, Westminster, CO

"Our family has been on a journey for ten years to find help for our struggling daughter. The general medical and educational communities offered us little hope. We refused to give up. Over the years, my daughter has been treated by numerous mainstream and non-traditional practitioners. In the past, we had seen minor improvements in our daughter's functioning. After two and a half years of Anna Buck's therapy, our daughter's growth academically and socially has been substantial. Our daughter is present for the first time!

A Journey of Hope gives a detailed description of the theories supporting Neuro-Developmental Delay therapy. It is also filled with encouraging and enlightening experiences of the families Anna has served over the years."

Nadine Fortune BSN, RN, Katy, TX

"We had tried many other solutions for our son, with very minimal steps forward, and lots of tears and frustration in the process. So by the time we found Anna, he was 17. I was associated with Christian Home Educators of Colorado at the time, and several people told me about Anna's House — how it helped their child, how easy-going Anna is. Additionally, her program only required 10-ish minutes a night, and only once-a-month visits to see Anna. We didn't know what God had planned for our son regarding academics since things weren't 'sticking.' But now our son is pursuing an engineering degree and has done very well taking community college courses. Thank you Anna!!!"

Julie D., Colorado

Acknowledgements

I am deeply grateful for my wonderful husband, Robert, who has been so patient with the time and energy that has consumed me with this project. Thank you, Kristin Wright-Bettner, for corrections and contributions that helped me more clearly put my thoughts into writing. Thank you to Nadine Fortune, who suggested the title.

And finally, thank you to the parents who so openly and graciously shared their children's stories. You made this book possible.

Introduction

Anna's House is a center for educational remediation beginning at the brain stem. Children and young people of all ages, from all over the United States (as well as a few from other countries), come with or without previous diagnoses (e.g., dyslexia, dysgraphia, ADD, ADHD, ASD — the list is endless). While *Anna's House* does not diagnose children, initial assessments determine the point of breakdown within each individual's central nervous system. We customize our remediation to begin at that point. As maturity of the central nervous system develops, overall maturity is observed. *Anna's House* does not identify difficulties and teach coping mechanisms or compensation techniques. The goal is to stimulate maturity of the central nervous system by recapturing earlier stages of development, beginning at the brain stem, so that children work through and beyond their difficulties.

> Anna's House does not identify difficulties and teach coping mechanisms or compensation techniques. The goal is to stimulate maturity of the central nervous system by recapturing earlier stages of development, beginning at the brain stem, so that children work through and beyond their difficulties.

Therapy at *Anna's House* considers an individual as a whole in order to determine the point of breakdown. When I consider a possible candidate for therapy beginning at the brain stem level, I first consider the child's history, beginning in the womb. Complications or trauma during pregnancy or birth may trigger neuro-developmental delay. Stress of any sort during pregnancy may affect the unborn child. Frequently I find identifiable stresses during pregnancy such as moving from one location to another, car accidents, job-related stress, marital difficulties, illness, death in the family, or various complications of the pregnancy itself. All sorts of unexpected traumas may surface during birth such as caesarian section, cord around the neck, lack of sufficient oxygen, long labor, stress during labor and birth, mishandling of the mother during labor and birth, unexpected stress to the mother during the birth process, etc. Premature births often point to delay in development. Trauma to a newborn or young child may also hinder maturity of the central nervous system, and what may not seem traumatic for one child might be highly traumatic to another. Each person perceives and experiences trauma to self differently. I have seen children traumatized from a slight fall that others would shake off. Either way, trauma is usually evident by a change in behavior. These types of experiences may, in turn, affect the child's development, later manifesting as behavioral and/or academic difficulties.

Functionality of systems in the body must also be considered. Speech, language and communication, gross and fine motor movements, cognitive function, balance and the vestibular system, and eye movements are evaluated collectively rather than individually in hopes of pointing to the place from which to begin. Add to that a continued presence of the primitive reflexes at the brain stem level, and signs point to breakdown at the foundation (brain stem). Neuro-Developmental Delay (NDD) therapy, or stimulation beginning at the brain stem, allows a child the opportunity to go back to earlier stages and stimulate development toward overall maturity of his or her central nervous system.

This book is about my experiences in working with children who initially showed signs of neuro-developmental delay and a need for stimulation at the brain stem level. At first, I was challenged by many in the health and educational fields that claimed children with behavioral and/or academic difficulties did not overcome them but needed to learn how to compensate and cope. They said some children might need to be medicated and most would require a diagnosis in order to get through life as best they could. I was also told that the brain stem could not be stimulated to bring about change, that individuals "live with what they are dealt at birth" (regarding the brain stem), unless future injury or illness alters its functionality.

During the last ten years, thinking in this area has drastically changed. We hear more and more about the primitive reflexes (brain stem functions) and the vestibular system (centered in the brain stem). In the last five years, medical doctors, psychologists, psychiatrists, occupational therapists, physical therapists, chiropractors, vision therapists, optometrists, teachers, special education teachers, school principals and others have witnessed changes in children I have worked with. Many have inquired about the work and brought their own children to *Anna's House*. Like me, they are parents who grieve for their children's sufferings, and the pain forces them to explore and research beyond common protocols. These are professionals who have investigated, recognized the value of NDD therapy, and witnessed maturity in their own children.

NDD therapy has not yet been acknowledged by the

health and medical field as a whole. The term "neuro-developmental therapy," as part of the health field, combines Physical Therapy, Occupational Therapy, and Speech Therapy. NDD therapy, however, stimulates development prior to the common protocol provided by traditional Occupational Therapy and Speech Therapy. For those whose careers lay in the medical or educational realms, this requires thinking "outside the box" of their education and experience; I have tremendous respect for those who can objectively investigate and step outside of traditional training and familiarity.

Many may disagree with what I share in this book, but these are my thoughts and observations. Having worked with hundreds of children in the last decade, I have seen firsthand that although children work through neuro-developmental delay differently, the most profound changes have come from stimulation of the brain stem, implemented slowly, carefully and individually. Every child is his own person and no two people experience this therapy in the same way. As a result, each child's therapy program is individualized so that even siblings generally do not follow the same pattern of progression. The stories are true, and enough people have witnessed changes in children to validate what I have to share. My desire is to see more and more children benefit from a developmental approach that begins at the brain stem. This is not a simple therapy, however, in that the process takes time and commitment; yet in many cases it also brings such maturity of the central nervous system that follow-up therapies are often not required. Parents who are committed to completion of the process are rewarded with seeing their children's potential blossom. For some children, their potential is appropriate maturity with slow academic performance; for others it is less extreme behavior and average or high academic performance; for others it is a miracle story of radical change. Instead of having had to learn coping mechanisms, numerous children reveal hidden talents and abilities. The process for every family is what many say they experience for the first time — a journey of hope.

TABLE OF CONTENTS

TABLE OF CONTENTS

PART 3: INTERACTIONS

TABLE OF CONTENTS

PART 4: JOURNEYS OF HOPE

PART 1:
THE FOUNDATION

Chapter 1

Getting to the Root of the Problem: The Brain Stem and Developmental Delay

An Epidemic of Diagnoses: Why?

Labels and diagnoses for learning difficulties and behavioral problems seem to be at an all-time high. The terms attention deficit disorder (ADD), attention deficit hyperactivity disorder (ADHD), dyslexia, autistic spectrum disorder, and others are tossed around in general conversation as an expected part of life. Our culture no longer seems surprised or concerned when a child is diagnosed with one thing or another. We ask why this has become epidemic, and there seems to be no definite answer. Children are diagnosed, put in special education programs, and medicated. Then the children, as well as their families, begin the process of coping with the disability.

Our culture has grown accustomed to the use of labels and diagnoses. But labels and diagnoses should be assigned with extreme caution. There are no clinical tests available to verify many of the common "disorders." Rather, a subjective gathering of symptoms is used to associate the behavior with the label of an official diagnosis. Interestingly, the official definitions for various disorders and their indicative lists of symptoms periodically change. Symptoms and clarifications of diagnoses are modified every so often by the American Psychiatric Association, authors of the Diagnostic and Statistical Manual of Mental Disorders (DSM 5 is the most recent edition). Health and mental health professionals largely rely on the DSM 5 for patient diagnoses. Once children are diagnosed, they typically carry their diagnoses for the remainder of their lives.

When I started my practice as a Neuro-Developmental Delay Therapist, I met children previously diagnosed with one overall "disability." Now I am routinely meeting children who have as many as nine or more diagnoses because each new label has been added to the previous one. I believe there is not only a danger of misdiagnosis but also of creating life-altering stigmas associated with bearing these labels. The assignment of a behavioral and/or learning diagnosis may potentially do more harm than good.

Many parents are raising concerns about the methods and procedures of diagnosing "disabilities." For some, it starts when their child enters school and all of a sudden has difficulty with reading or writing or math, or shows behavioral problems that are brought to the parents' attention by the teacher. Parents have shared with me concerns about the pressure they receive from school specialists to go along with whatever is recommended, and many times parents have doubts that the recommendations are truly best for their child. I frequently hear stories from parents about school staff suggesting use of psychotropic drugs — medications that chemically affect the central nervous system at the cellular level and alter moods and behavior.

Having observed children on psychotropic drugs such as Ritalin, Adderall, Risperdal, and many, many others, I have become more and more concerned about this growing trend to medicate children with behavioral and/or attention problems. In general, the observable side effects of these drugs have been alarming. I have seen children develop tremors and twitches while on these drugs; when they stopped taking the drugs, the tremors and twitches decreased or disappeared. I have seen children sit and stare wide-eyed at a wall during a drugged state. Some children become aggressive and hostile while using these drugs, and our society increasingly experiences evidence of such violence. By far, the most common concern voiced from parents has been that their children have lost their personalities. While they may have become calmer and less reactive, their "aliveness" is gone.

Teachers, coaches, and adults who frequently work with children may recommend use of medications, suggesting that the drugs will help children with attention deficit and/or hyperactivity. My experience suggests that, in truth, the use of drugs is to make these children more manageable and tolerable. In the classroom, children who show attention difficulties and are easily distracted but do *not* disrupt or distract others are generally not referred for drugs. Psychotropic medications are habitually recommended for children who need to be controlled or less disruptive toward those around them. I rarely agree, however, that these children require medication because, having worked with these types of children, I have seen profound changes come without medication.

Most of us have observed family situations in which lack of discipline, behavioral accountability, or use of the word "no" have directly contributed to negative behavior in children. In some cases, however, behavior problems are not due to a lack of discipline. In fact, discipline is ineffective. There are children who react involuntarily so that "controlling" them or managing their behavior is nearly impossible. I have observed children who previously reacted involuntarily such that they could not be managed, yet they matured through NDD therapy, and are now capable of appropriate behavior. They become more responsive and less reactive, able to control their behavior and emotions. As the ability to demonstrate self-control emerges, appropriate accountability needs to be applied. If parents and teachers do not recognize this change, however, and adjust their expectations and discipline accordingly, the child's behavior may not improve. What was previously a developmental concern may later become a lack-of-discipline issue. NDD therapy has stimulated maturity in many of these children so that they become ready for discipline and consequences.

More and more parents are seeking answers outside of the general medical and educational realms. Now, more than ever, brain therapies of all sorts are surfacing, all offering answers and services for children with behavioral and learning difficulties. Parents are ever seeking for something that will enable their children to overcome their struggles.

As a parent of a struggling child, I fought against the system and refused to allow my child to be diagnosed. We tried numerous programs, interventions, and therapies. Yet all the while I struggled mentally with the random approach of wandering from therapy to therapy. Gaps were not being filled, and I wrestled with and searched for what might lie at the root of it all. Once I learned about normal development of the central nervous system, "the lights came on," and for the first time I felt a flood of relief, understanding, and hope that my daughter could truly get past her struggles. My message to parents of struggling children is to have hope, be encouraged, and keep reading.

The following describes the central nervous system — the significance of its function in early development and how it may affect later maturity related to behavior and academics.

Development of the Central Nervous System: An Overview

The central nervous system normally develops in a strategic and purposeful manner so that one stage triggers the next. Each stage is dependent upon the previous stage for effective maturity. What a baby does in the womb affects infant development, which affects toddlerhood, early childhood, and every age beyond. A child's experiences during pregnancy, birth, the early months, and the first few years provide valuable clues and signs regarding appropriate and natural development of the central nervous system.

"Normal" children do not crawl or creep before learning to hold their heads up off the floor; newborns are expected to react with an infant startle from sudden movement, sound, or light; infants do not yet track with their eyes. An infant is not expected to process sensory information (e.g., interpret sounds, textures, or tastes and reach an accurate conclusion), and we would never think of trying to desensitize sensory experiences in a child that age. They simply react and we understand that and accept it. Toddlers mimic sounds before they begin to say words. Parents would think it ridiculous if speech therapy were recommended for their young toddler prior to the age in which speech development begins. In my experience, behavior and learning problems frequently point to these very early stages of development. Specific and appropriate intervention for a given individual should be based on the normal pattern of development. Therapy programs, therefore, are potentially most helpful when these delayed stages are recognized and considered first.

Signs of delay in the central nervous system's development are observable and identifiable because they affect children in several and varying areas: behavior, emotions, sensory processing, eye movements for reading and writing, auditory processing, body awareness, balance, motor movements, speech and articulation, and finally, school readiness. One child might show sensitivities to touch, behavior that is highly emotional, and speech impairment. Another child might be smart but struggle academically and show vision difficulties as well. Older children with developmental delay might demonstrate inconsistent and questionable behaviors. Parents and I meet to discuss these conflicting behaviors and the stages of development they represent — part of a child might still be functioning similarly to an infant or toddler, other areas might be like that of a two-year old, and other areas, often including intellect, are age-appropriate. The child is confused inside his own body. As I observe the child, I am usually able to identify the age level of the behavior while ignoring the child's physical age. This becomes an eye-opener for parents, and they begin to look at their child a bit differently and with less frustration.

When a child manifests signs of delay in development of the central nervous system, the logical and natural first step should be to stimulate the central nervous system where development begins and where breakdown occurred. Instead of separating the symptoms and treating them individually through multiple therapies, the overall cause should first be determined. The common-sense approach is to respond to a child's needs based on normal development. I encourage parents to step back and observe their child a bit before randomly pursuing one therapy after another. This should not be a helter-skelter approach. I, too, was a parent who searched for answers and sought opinions and evaluations. Once I learned the process of development of the central nervous system, beginning in the womb, I understood the value and importance of looking at behavioral and learning difficulties from a logical, strategic standpoint based on how a body normally develops. The pattern has been laid within the central nervous system of each human being, and all we need to do is follow the process. It almost seems too simplistic.

> Instead of separating the symptoms and treating them individually through multiple therapies, the overall cause should first be determined.

As a baby develops inside his mother's womb, his central nervous system develops from the bottom up. In other words, the first movements are generated from the spinal cord, followed by spontaneous or involuntary movements from the brain stem. Within several months following birth, controlled movements are generated from the midbrain and the cerebellum. Later, reasoning and processing develop from the cortex. The brain develops from the spinal cord to the brain stem and then to the upper levels of the brain.[1]

The House Analogy

I have come to loosely describe development and

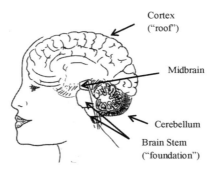

Cortex ("roof")

Midbrain

Cerebellum

Brain Stem ("foundation")

dysfunction of the central nervous system by analogizing it to construction of a house. When problems are found with the roof, window casings, or door jambs, repeated attempts at repairs are done in vain if problems with the foundation are the cause. We must first take care of the foundation and then, if other areas still need repair, we pursue them in proper order. Similarly, the brain stem is the foundation of the central nervous system and later maturity depends upon a stable foundation.

If a child shows breakdown and dysfunction in the brain stem (the foundation), multiple therapies that target other areas of function, as in the analogy of the house, become repetitive and leave gaps. For example, I have been increasingly hearing the term "executive dysfunction" applied to struggling children. This simply means that function at the cognitive level (thinking, understanding, learning, and remembering) is impaired. Using the house analogy, cognitive function is the "roof." "Executive" function might very likely be dysfunctional due to breakdown that occurred in earlier stages of development. It is therefore imperative to determine the point of breakdown instead of assuming remediation should start at the "roof." These children often show breakdown at the foundation. Many professionals push for compensation and coping techniques at the cognitive level, and I stress the need to wait and watch for changes based on normal and natural development during and following NDD therapy. Once the "foundation" of the central nervous system becomes secure, then interventions for improved cognitive function, if needed, have greater chance for success. So far, this message has been poorly received. I surmise that this may be because the concept of going back to early stages of development and stimulating the central nervous system to initiate maturity is still unfamiliar to many.

The most profound changes I have observed in children with developmental delay come when they are carefully stimulated so that experiences they need to repeat or retrace trigger natural development. Therapy at the brain stem level is that process such that maturity of the central nervous system is initiated. Creeping on hands and knees may easily come to mind as many children skip that stage and need to go back through it again. It may start long before that, however. Some children still struggle with being able to hold their heads up off the floor or sit without back support, or comfortably roll from their tummies to their backs and vice versa. There are numerous stages of development, and many children need to go back to early stages that should have been experienced within the first few months of birth. These early stages are vital to later development. I think of the results of this process as a domino effect — maturity at the brain stem level triggers development of the midbrain, cerebellum and cortex. Just as construction of a house begins at the foundation and moves toward the roof, maturity of the central nervous system begins at the brain stem and progresses to higher functions that prepare a child for school and learning. This is why NDD therapy (beginning at the brain stem) should be the first consideration when a child shows dysfunction across several systems.

Manifestations of Developmental Delay Beginning at the Brain Stem Level

A variety of specific indicators point to dysfunction of the brain stem. Because all the sensory systems in the body must first pass through areas of the brain stem for processing, dysfunction at the brain stem can cause difficulties in a number of areas, as previously mentioned: balance and coordination, behavior and emotions, auditory processing and speech, the visual system, vestibular and sensory interpretations. Careful observation of children with struggles in these areas often shows behavior consistent with the developmental age(s) in which parts of them seem to be "stuck." These areas can be observed and tested; the information gathered is objective and measurable. A brief introduction follows and greater detail will be presented throughout this book.

Body Positions

Many children continue well beyond the appropriate age to position themselves in infant-like positions. During my initial visit with a child, I repeatedly and randomly ask them to lie on their backs and on their tummies. It is not unusual to see, again and again, the same child lie down with arms or legs in infantile positions.

This photo was taken within two hours of my granddaughter's birth. Notice her elbows are bent and her hands are in fists. This is a common infant position. A newborn's hands often remain near their face. I 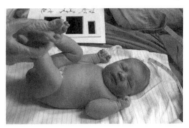 see this same position in many older children (including teens). Each time I ask them to lie on their backs, the elbows bend, the fingers curl loosely or tightly to form fists, and the hands rest near the face.

Sleeping positions in infants, when not on their tummies, may closely resemble a fetal position.  Gradually, over time, the infant should begin to stretch out in varying positions. The photo to the left was taken when my granddaughter was five days old. Notice her back is not as rounded as it would be if she were in a full fetal position, but the legs and arms are curled in resemblance of a fetal position. I have worked with a number of children who assume a fetal position when under stress. It is not unusual for me to watch a child in my office curl up into his or her mother's lap and adjust into this position. Many older children continue to sleep in a fetal position.

At two months of age, my granddaughter was able to easily lift her head up off the floor when she lay on her tummy. When her head lifted, so did her legs and feet. This is technically referred to as a Landau position, reaction, or reflex. The position is considered part of normal development in infants during the first few months after birth. I frequently see this same position in older children, however. If they have enough muscle tone to lift their heads up off the floor (some are unable to lift their heads and others do so weakly), the legs

involuntarily lift as well and the position is nearly identical to the position in this photo. I have seen older children roll from their backs to their tummies and as their tummies reach the floor, the body automatically moves into this position: the head stiffly remains elevated, the legs and feet are rigidly held in a raised position, and the back arches.

At age 20 months, my granddaughter's arms sometimes rested near her head when she slept, and at other times they rested down near her sides. The legs often splayed so that the toes met at midline, as in the photo to the right. Within a short time, her legs straightened during sleep so that the angle behind each knee expanded. One or both legs might bend, but slightly. Her feet stretched out, and her sleeping positions started to resemble those of older individuals, including adults.

Interestingly, I occasionally see the leg position shown in the photo in older children. I have asked children and teens to lie on their backs and some will, each time, drop their legs into this position. Their legs easily fall outward to the sides, but struggle with lifting and crossing midline. They usually show limited hip rotation and when standing, one leg often bends at the knee and leans in toward the other leg. These same children typically have awkward gaits.

Primitive Reflexes

The continued presence of several of the primitive reflexes usually validates observed body positions and behavior. Primitive reflexes are involuntary movements initiated at the brain stem level, such as an infant startle (Moro Reflex). They begin in utero and continue through about age one. Their purpose is to work together to help a child adjust to life outside the womb and to provide fundamental preparation for later voluntary movements. While they do not collectively emerge, or later withdraw at the same time, their workings overlap. (The order in which the reflexes are presented in this book is based on what I have observed to be a common path of withdrawal.) Within the first year of normal development, they should withdraw as postural reflexes begin to emerge. The postural reflexes emerge at the midbrain-cerebellum level and should be retained for life because they allow mature posture for sitting, standing, and walking. A child who retains several primitive reflexes typically does not experience full emergence of the postural reflexes.

Eye Movements

The continued presence of primitive reflexes in older children affects development of eye movements. One hundred percent of the children I work with demonstrate some sort of struggle with eye movements, such as difficulty with convergence, tracking, or hand-eye tracking. In normal development, natural withdrawal (inhibition) of the primitive reflexes stimulates development of eye movements. I watch for eye movements to improve naturally as we stimulate normal development at the brain stem level. I have seen amazing improvements in children who were diagnosed with "lazy eye," crossed eyes, and other complications, but only if those children did not previously experience eye surgery.

The Vestibular System

Vestibular function affects posture and balance as well as the visual and auditory systems. The nucleus of the vestibular system resides in the brain stem, where vestibular input is processed and messages are relayed between the brain and the body. When the vestibular system is dysfunctional, responses within the nervous system become inconsistent and inaccurate. One hundred percent of the children I work with show some degree of vestibular dysfunction. Specific vestibular stimulation at the brain stem level has been shown to trigger withdrawal of the primitive reflexes, and exercise movements that stimulate inhibition of the primitive reflexes have been shown to trigger improved vestibular function.

The Vagus Nerve

In my experience, children who show developmental delay beginning at the brain stem level sometimes have one or more physical complaints as well. They may have allergies, asthma, a low-functioning immune system, skin ailments, digestion disorders, and problems with bed wetting or involuntary urination. While the therapy does not target these physical conditions, improvements have been observed.

The vagus nerve, also known as the pneumogastric nerve ("pneumo" refers to the lungs and "gastric" refers to the stomach) or 10th cranial nerve, is part of the parasympathetic nervous system. After the sympathetic nervous system excites and stirs things up the parasympathetic nervous system helps to bring things back into balance. While the sympathetic nervous system may engage a fight or flight reaction, a mature parasympathetic nervous system should help the body return to homeostasis. Like a highway, the vagus nerve begins in the brain stem. It travels around and down, winding its way through the body, and branches into side roads along the way. It interrelates with other cranial nerves and then travels to the heart, trachea, lungs, esophagus, stomach, abdominal blood vessels, liver, pancreas, intestines, rectum, kidneys, bladder and genitalia. It helps regulate heart rate and contraction, breathing, blood pressure, sweating, peristalsis (digestion of food), urination and defecation, as well muscle movements in the mouth related to speech.

Stimulation of the brain stem through small, regulated movements has shown physical improvements regarding bodily functions in many children. Parents, physicians, and optometrists have commented on improvements in areas such as breathing and asthma conditions, regulation of body temperature, skin conditions, digestion, allergies, bladder and rectum control, eye movements, speech and language, etc. Stimulation at the brain stem level seems to affect the workings of the vagus nerve differently amongst individuals and in varying degrees within each person.

Auditory Processing

Children with developmental delay originating from the brain stem often show some degree of difficulty with auditory processing — how the brain processes auditory information. This makes sense because vestibular function affects the auditory system. In normal development, the vestibular system develops at a faster rate than the auditory system; if the vestibular system is dysfunctional, it follows that the auditory system may also be dysfunctional.

The Impact of it All: A Personal Story

Dysfunction at the brain stem level, then, must be

considered when higher levels of function show impairment or delay. Once it has been established that breakdown is rooted at the brain stem level, NDD therapy provides stimulation at that level so that maturity of the central nervous system may begin. NDD (Neuro-Developmental Delay) therapy is a process of inhibition (that is, withdrawal) of the primitive reflexes, emergence of the postural reflexes, and stimulation of the vestibular system at the brain stem level. Remediation that begins at the brain stem level may naturally remediate dysfunction elsewhere.

My own daughter, at age 18, suffered from irrational fears and could not be soothed, much like a newborn. Physically, she demonstrated toddler-like movements when it came to balance and motor skills. Her writing skills were at kindergarten level, and her reading ability was at the level of a third grader. Once I recognized the need to stimulate her central nervous system at the brain stem, I was able to adapt to her needs, and my own frustration dropped phenomenally. As her central nervous system began to mature while employing NDD therapy, I was able to observe successive developmental stages as she experienced them. Balance naturally developed. She started to dance and spin like a three-year old. She progressed to the stage in which she was able to hop on a bicycle and ride down the street. By stimulating the central nervous system at the earliest level of development, changes gradually became automatic, and gaps began to close. All of a sudden reading blossomed, followed by writing. At age 20, she fell in love with coloring and spent hours coloring in book after book (due to lack of hand-eye coordination, she had never been able to color inside the lines, nor had she previously shown any interest in coloring). Soon that phase passed, and she moved into the next. I realized she was advancing through phases of earlier development in which she either needed more time or the opportunity to experience specific stages for the first time. I swallowed my pride and decided to watch and trust. I was richly rewarded. Her story, like the stories of many others, demonstrates remarkable growth and continued maturity that resulted from stimulation at the brain stem level.

Chapter 2

There's a Beach at the End of the Waves: Behavior, Emotions, and NDD Therapy — What to Expect

Overview: The Importance of Patience and Customization

The process of NDD therapy is not easy; neither is it quick. Although a few children I have worked with completed programs in a year or less, the average length of time is 18-24 months and more extreme cases may take two, three, or more years depending on the severity. Growth often continues for the following several years. My daughter's NDD therapy program was about a two-year process, yet maturity advanced and was noticeably obvious through the following seven years. This is a natural by-product because when natural development is stimulated, it should carry on. We expect children to grow and mature. When a child shows delay and is then stimulated from the point of breakdown, we hope to see the natural process "kick in" and then continue normally, hopefully without further intervention. My daughter's ongoing maturity was easily recognizable as the changes in the years following

> Growth often continues for the following several years.

therapy showed abilities, reasoning, logic, and vestibular functions that I had never seen previously. This may not be as obvious, however, to parents of younger children because natural maturity has reached appropriate age level at a younger age. Maturation, nevertheless, should carry on after a child's NDD therapy program ends.

The process of the therapy can be fairly smooth, or it can be extremely rough. Every child is different, and what one family experiences is not necessarily what other families experience. It is interesting, however, that similar patterns of change can be observed. The brain stem is responsible for basic, vital life functions such as breathing, heartbeat, and blood pressure. These areas may be noticeably affected, especially soon after starting the therapy. I am not surprised, therefore, when at first I observe or hear about changes in regulation of body temperature, breathing, sensory sensitivities (light, sound, taste, touch) and moods. Some children immediately show growth in maturity, body awareness, eye contact, balance, and verbal expression. Occasionally academics improve right away. While a few children might unexpectedly start reading, others might become interested in reading for the first time or show improvement in reading. A few children suddenly progress in math. Most children, however, do not show considerable academic improvement until later on in their therapy.

During the first two to three months of NDD therapy, I frequently hear parents say, "I can't place exactly what's different, but something is." When I suggest, "Do you think maybe he just seems to fit inside his body better?" they have consistently said, "Yes! That's it!" Some parents have shared that their child seems more hyper or overly busy with body movements. As I watch the child move about in my office, I am often able to see that what used to be flailing body movements are now organized and planned actions. The child is playing with his or her balance. Parents may be discouraged, however, because the movements are still those of younger children. I then explain that I am encouraged — because I commonly see older children progress from random flailing about to organized body movements that resemble three-year-old children. This is developmental progress! This is how children mature in normal development. Regardless of their physical age, these children need to recapture those earlier stages of body movement and balance.

School can be difficult during the beginning stages of NDD therapy. Children in public school are often already in special education programs. Sometimes the school's interventions are counterproductive to NDD therapy because coping mechanisms are taught and implemented. While schools want to provide services they hope will help, I encourage parents to bide their time. In my experience, this is understandably frustrating for most teachers and specialists in the school system. During the past few years, I have worked with several phenomenal teachers who offered support, encouragement, and their classroom observations. A team effort between parents, teachers, and *Anna's House* has proven to be most beneficial. These children often experience high stress levels at school, and what they need most is less stress. When they are pushed to perform at levels they sense they cannot achieve, one of two things generally occurs. Either they show extreme anxiety that manifests as behavioral problems, or they show signs of despair. It is not unusual to hear a child in this state repeatedly say, "I am stupid." What they need most is time and the opportunity to let their bodies catch up to being physiologically ready to learn.

A child with neuro-developmental delay usually behaves much younger than his physical age. One little girl I knew was chronologically seven, but developmentally she was more like a newborn. Along with NDD therapy, the mother started activities with her that a parent would typically do with a child under six months of age. Within a few months, the child made significant strides. Another mother realized that while her son was physically seven, developmentally he was closer to age three. As a homeschooling mom, she changed his "schoolwork" to activities she had already been initiating with her three-and-a-half-year old, and right away frustration levels dropped for both mother and son. I think parents and teachers harbor fears that if they pull back on academics to the level of the child's developmental age, the child will never progress beyond that level. I have never seen this to be the case. As long as parents continue working with their child through the developmental stages, maturity comes according to their potential. As the parent of a child who struggled severely, I live with regret that I pushed my daughter academically instead of waiting until she was developmentally ready. It was due to that same fear — if I did not push, she might never progress. During and after NDD therapy, her reading, math, writing, and everyday

> I think parents and teachers harbor fears that if they pull back on academics to the level of the child's developmental age, the child will never progress beyond that level.

functioning blossomed on their own beyond my wildest dreams.

As children progress through NDD therapy, I listen to parents' observations and look for clues that show a child's readiness for learning. I remember a mother sharing at one visit that in the two previous weeks, her son had begun naming the letters of the alphabet and making some of the sounds. I was surprised that she would see this so soon, but I quickly tested a few areas and said, "Yes, start teaching him to read!" Other times, I encourage parents to keep waiting, or keep school work slow and steady, because the child is not quite ready.

The process of primitive reflex inhibition varies among individuals. No two children progress in exactly the same manner. An overall stereotypical pattern can be seen, but, just as in normal development, each person has his or her own individualized style. Just as the reflexes do not all emerge in the womb at one time and then inhibit collectively all at one time in normal development, they do not inhibit or withdraw all at once during NDD therapy. Neither do they necessarily withdraw sequentially — first one reflex, then another, then another. I have observed that many children show inhibition of two or three reflexes at about the same time. The reflexes that typically emerge later also characteristically withdraw later. Part of the job of an NDD therapist is to find the pattern of withdrawal in given individuals and match it with applicable exercise movements.

NDD therapy consists of simple, physical movements that are chosen specifically for given individuals and their particular needs. Because the process of NDD therapy varies among individuals, the exercise movements are not based on a "cookie cutter" process. The exercises assigned are generally one at a time, carried out one time each day. This means it takes, on average, less than ten minutes per day to do the therapy. One child may need only one exercise movement for many months; a similar child may require several different exercise movements during the same period of time. I have learned the value of respecting the process within each individual and appreciating the need for discerning the specific mode of progression within each person.

Because behavior and emotions are heavily intertwined with NDD therapy, I have addressed them specifically as part of the entire process. Some children never show behavioral or emotional instability, but most do to some extent. The experience for many families is one in which behavior and/or emotions heighten for a time and then settle so that stability becomes the norm. Others show heightened behavior and/or emotions throughout their NDD program.

Behavior and Emotions

Children might start acting babyish and silly, others sob uncontrollably and without cause, and others become intensely angry. I observe children that stay in one mode of behavior or emotions throughout much of their therapy program while others transition from one phase of behavior or emotions into others. For these, the behaviors and/or emotions manifested may change, almost like stages, such as from silliness to sobbing, to screaming and yelling, to anger. As long as parents persist with their commitment to the therapy, we do see the behavior and emotions settle. The settled behavior should be demonstrated by increased self-control; the child is able to think about the consequences before acting out. The child's personality becomes evident in the process. The difference becomes behavior by choice instead of involuntary reactions.

The emotional ups and downs children experience as they work through changes at the brain stem level vary widely. Parents commonly struggle with understanding and responding to what they see. Some parents see a calmness that settles almost immediately. Most are not that fortunate. I try to encourage parents to look at their child's immediate behavior and think, "What age does the behavior seem to match?" Usually, they can tie the behavior to a specific age such as two or three. Some parents initially complain about immature, childish, or silly behavior. Others see melt-downs and temper tantrums that increase in frequency or intensity at first and then calm down. Rarely does a child show both reduced frequency and intensity of negative behavior simultaneously; usually one decreases and then the other.

Typical initial feedback from parents about their children's behavior includes justification of misbehavior, inappropriate laughing, pestering siblings, irrational sobbing, argumentativeness, and defiance. Yet at about the same time, I frequently hear that more awareness of inappropriate behavior surfaces — remorse or embarrassment can be detected.

Verbal communication usually emerges as well and is often poorly or negatively spoken, similar to that of a three-year old just learning self-expression. Parents have to teach their three-year-olds appropriate manners of expression, and often an older child who begins to verbalize needs to learn appropriate expression either again, or for the very first time. I commonly visit with children and teens who were initially either clueless or nonchalant about their inappropriate behavior. Not long into their NDD therapy program, they talk more openly about what they recognize in themselves as being inappropriate and express a desire to change. Some apologize or show improved articulation of frustrations, fears, and anxieties.

While the negative behavior may seem uglier than ever at first, positive changes may surface in physical areas such as coordination and balance. Many children start to jump rope, hop on one foot, or ride a bike more naturally. Some parents occasionally notice calmer behavior, while others may see it later during the therapy.

In my experience, many children go through periods in which behavior and/or emotions mimic pendulum swings. Reactions are extreme and parents are concerned and may experience alarm and frustration. Then the child's behavior might swing in the opposite direction, equally extreme. When it swings back in the first direction, it is less extreme, even if just slightly less. Over time, the swings are less dramatic; moderation and more normal behaviors are observable.

The following individual stories demonstrate the variation between different children's experiences, and the overlapping mix of positive and (initially) negative changes in behavior that are often observed during the course of an NDD therapy program.

Rachel

Rachel, nearly nine years old when I met her, got off to a rocky start with her first NDD exercise. Her parents noticed that immediately following the exercise each night, she needed and wanted to be cradled. Her daily behavior consisted of deliberate disobedience, complete lack of self-control, and spitting on her siblings. One positive change was that she began to comfortably tip her head back when swallowing her vitamins and when rinsing her hair in the shower.

During Rachel's second month of NDD therapy, she started verbalizing her frustration. She yelled, cried, threw things, and was less patient with her siblings. Her parents said they thought there was some improvement over the previous month in that her behavior seemed less "off the wall" and moments of self-control had appeared.

Rachel's third month showed more emotional behavior. She overreacted with screaming at the slightest provocation. She started punishing herself such as sending herself to bed after a reprimand. She continued to struggle with being separated from one or both parents, displayed general clumsiness, and started sleepwalking. Her exercise had not changed, but her response to it did. One night she curled up into a fetal position and cried for a time. When this happens, I suspect that something in the central nervous system has just been triggered toward positive change. With Rachel, her reading improved. She found it more enjoyable, and it began to "click." I retested Rachel, noting improvements regarding inhibition of the primitive reflexes and better eye convergence.

The next month showed continued positive changes. Rachel no longer needed her bedroom light on at night; she was comfortable with a small nightlight. She no longer required medication for her asthma. Swimming improved. She sought sleep when stressed. Overall, though, Rachel's parents described her behavior as still showing immaturity and clumsiness.

Two months later, Rachel was back to wanting her bedroom light on at night, although it was short-lived, and she again became content without a light. Various fears were high — the dark, monsters, being kidnapped, being alone, and insects. On the positive side, she wanted to be of service to others — set the table, wash the dishes, etc. She also showed increased responsibility such as taking showers, washing her hair, and completing chores on her own. She sought an outlet for calming herself — jumping on her trampoline. During this period, Rachel's attention span continued to be low, memory was still poor, and loud noises still bothered her.

Nearly a year after starting NDD therapy, Rachel started riding her bicycle and showing more confidence in general. She played well with seven-year-old children even though she was nearly 10. Her fears had decreased, but they did not completely go away. Sixteen months after starting therapy, Rachel showed tremendous changes in maturity. Her behavior was improved and her appetite was better; she offered to help her mother clean, showed some improvement in her ability to follow directions, and cleaned her bedroom on her own.

Rachel had completed the listening therapy and was nearly finished with NDD therapy two years after she started. Her parents shared observations of tremendous improvements in sensory processing, social interactions, balance, and motor movements. Her behavior had become age-appropriate. I measured tremendous maturity of the central nervous system — the primitive reflexes were nearly fully inhibited, and eye movements were smooth.

Caleb

Caleb, seven-and-a-half when we met, showed considerable developmental delay. Other than general immaturity, he struggled with hyperactivity, attention, listening, social behavior, body awareness, and academics. Because he was taking Adderall (a psychotropic drug), however, overall progress was extremely slow. Nevertheless, within six months of starting NDD therapy, he received his first award at school for having not gotten into trouble once during an entire week. A year after starting NDD therapy, he showed good behavior in one-on-one situations but was generally unmotivated academically. Consequences did not affect him. While his behavior was emotional with a lot of yelling, he also showed immediate remorse. He often screamed, yelled, cried, and slammed his bedroom door. He would then recover within about 30-40 minutes after being alone. The outbursts lessened over time, and he was able to stop taking Adderall. His teachers were impressed with the behavioral changes and academic progress he made in the subsequent two years.

Angela

Angela was a girl who was highly volatile and instantly reactive in an aggressive manner, especially toward her siblings. She was strong athletically, but academics suffered. Her behavior was quite immature for a nine-and-a-half-year-old; she often spoke softly and in a babyish voice. Soon after she started NDD therapy, her emotions escalated and I heard about an aggressive incident on the school playground. During the following few months, her emotions were like a roller coaster in that she would be highly emotional one day, yet show more control and restraint on other days. On the other hand, math started to improve. One of the biggest changes was her lack of desire to wear her glasses all the time. After an exam, her optometrist noticed tremendous improvements in eye movements, changed her prescription, and asked what kind of therapy Angela was doing. The primary concern for Angela transitioned from her aggressive outbursts to wishing she approached academics and chores with a better attitude. Her behavior had become less reactive and more self-controlled. Her family was able to see more of her genuine personality without the extreme, reactionary behaviors.

Sara

Sara was a teenager who struggled with academics and low self-esteem. Her angry outbursts at home concerned her parents because she had become aggressive, hitting her mother and her brother. After seven months of NDD therapy, her mother shared that Sara had become more successful at school (straight As), more organized, and more confident. Her daily homework showed completion in a timely manner. While her angry outbursts continued, her mother said they were significantly less frequent. Interestingly, Sara and her mother both agreed that as long as she did her assigned NDD exercise daily, she was noticeably happier the next day. When she skipped her exercise even just one day, she was easily triggered toward angry outbursts. As she continued with her NDD therapy program, her mother described her behavior as more stable and more like a "typical" teenager.

Behavior usually gets worse before it gets better. I encourage parents to look for small, subtle, positive changes. With the discouraging behavior, good things come as well. This is a hard and challenging time. I remind parents to watch the behavior and think, "What age is this behavior showing?" instead of telling their child, "Act your age." Children respond better if treated according to the age of their behavior instead of according to their physical age.

While behavioral and emotional variation during NDD therapy is to some extent unavoidable, some techniques and approaches can help ease the process.

Anger

Many children experience a period of intense anger. I encourage parents to help their child find an outlet for releasing their anger so that it does not build up and explode or, on the other hand, become suppressed. Usually, physical outlets help tremendously. My daughter held a pencil over a large stack of paper and drew hard, pounding circles as intensely as she chose for as long as she desired. Over time, she spent less time grinding the pencil and gradually found she no longer needed or desired to pummel pencils through paper. Children need an avenue that is harmless, such as punching a bag, jumping on a trampoline, running, or riding a bicycle — anything that helps release the anger and brings relief to the child. One father shared that on one occasion his son reached this point of extreme anger in front of friends and relatives and, as a result, embarrassed himself with his own behavior. The father started observing more closely, and as soon as he noticed his son's anger beginning to

> Children respond better if treated according to the age of their behavior instead of according to their physical age.

surface, he interrupted the activity and suggested that his son join him for a quick walk outside. He helped his son release his anger before it fully flared and spared him the agony of embarrassment.

Temper tantrums sometimes mimic that of toddlers. It is difficult to make the connection that a child is developmentally a toddler when he or she is over five feet tall, but when parents observe carefully, they realize that is exactly what they are seeing.

One adopted teenager, nearly 18, had been diagnosed with ADD, sensory integration disorder and learning disabilities. Shortly after she started NDD therapy, her mother said she reacted more explosively and showed extreme anger. Every day included a fight of some sort. Yet she liked her NDD exercise and said it felt relaxing. Within the first four months, she became less volatile, was better able to focus in the classroom, and thought her writing had improved. Eye movements showed substantial improvement. A month later, she was retested at school and moved from a special education plan (IEP) to a 504 (she no longer needed a special education plan, but still benefited from a few accommodations within the regular coursework). Her mother said her behavior overall showed increased maturity.

I remember one teenager who performed well in school but was overly emotional at home. She insisted on her mother's help with homework but then yelled at her when her mother tried to help. When she made a mistake, she tore up her paper and started over. Homework became a long, drawn-out process that consumed the family's evenings, primarily because her behavior disrupted the entire household. School nights were emotionally draining. As she continued with NDD therapy, she grew less emotional about her school work and began completing her homework independently and in less time. After several months, her mother said they finally had peace in their home.

Some children repeatedly curse (it may not be a reflection of what they hear at home). I have observed several children, boys in particular, who all of a sudden stop the cursing sometime during NDD therapy. Parents have commented that cursing subsided for a while, resurfaced, and followed this back-and-forth pattern for a time before finally ceasing. (Children generally continue to curse, however, if they frequently hear it at home.)

Fears

Extreme reactions to fears are common. While some children show a complete lack of fear, others are overly fearful. Parents often tell me their children show a lack of appropriate fear of strangers, heights, or dangers. Their children will do anything or try anything without regard for their own safety. Other children are the opposite. They seem to fear absolutely everything. These children frequently show no or limited eye contact, may not talk to anyone other than a family member, or might whisper softly so that they cannot be heard. Other children show mixed extremes. They may be overly fearful in some situations and lack appropriate fear at other times.

Common fears in children I have observed include separation anxiety, being acknowledged as individuals (through eye contact or direct questions), moving objects, the dark, imaginary beings, nightmares, TV shows and/or movies, animals, insects, loud or unfamiliar noises, and being touched or moved against their will. The list of fears is endless, and I learn of new ones regularly. It is not the fear itself that concerns me most but the state of the child as a result of his or her fears.

Many children have a fear of closing their eyes. I have heard children say, "I can't hear the story if my eyes are closed," or, "Everything disappears when my eyes close." The statement that can bring me to tears just thinking about it is: "I disappear when I close my eyes." Imagine thinking your existence ceases, or you somehow disappear into a black hole each time you close your eyes! This can definitely affect response to separation from one or both parents, or behavior at bedtime — a child's willingness to go to bed, or to sleep in his or her own bed. Just as it is incredibly disturbing to see this fear in a child, it is equally exciting when the child has matured to the point of no longer fearing to close his eyes. My daughter is one of many I have known who initially thought the world remained but she disappeared when she closed her eyes. I cannot begin to imagine the horror of such a feeling, and I am forever grateful that she no longer experiences such terror.

As the primitive reflexes withdraw in children, I appreciate hearing that the extremes become more stable and less pendulum-like; a child no longer runs up to strangers and asks to be their friend; a child realizes if he jumps off the ledge he might get hurt; a child knows he should not run out into the street to escape a bee. Likewise, I thoroughly enjoy watching and listening as a child is finally able to look me in the eye and tell me about a personal experience without twitching, rocking, or hesitation. I delight in listening to children who have come through their fears and are able to uninhibitedly and excitedly tell me their story.

Hyperactivity

Many parents describe their children as being hyperactive. When I meet with these children, I might see true hyperactivity or behavior demonstrative of a deeper or different issue. To some parents, restlessness or fidgetiness is hyperactivity; to others, busyness with the body is hyperactivity; to still others, high energy is hyperactivity. "Hyperactivity" is a generalized term that I have found needs to be narrowed down to a precise and accurate description. In general, it means a state of being abnormally active. This is subjective, however, and being "abnormally active" may stem from a variety of sources.

Children who show neuro-developmental delay may struggle with "hyperactivity" for one or more reasons. It may be the result of a complete lack of body awareness or understanding of how their own bodies fit in space. It seems their bodies are constantly flailing about in one way or another. Through considerable observation, one can see that it is almost as if the child is in a constant search to find himself. Occasionally I describe this type of child as being like a balloon that might float away if someone did not grab onto the string to anchor or rein him in. On a few occasions, teachers have called asking for suggestions about how to manage a child like this in the classroom. I remember one boy in particular whose teacher and I talked about ways to define this boy's space for him until he became able to do it for himself. We agreed to try having her apply masking tape to the floor as the perimeter of an area that included his desk and chair — as much space as she could willingly provide. Then she told the boy that his space was inside those lines. Anytime during the school day when he became overly hyper and was "bouncing off the walls," she said, "E..., find your space." Each time, he consistently put himself inside the taped boundaries.

Another teacher provided a rug for a boy in her class because the students spent a lot of time on the floor in groups. When his arms or legs wandered, she said, "J..., you have to stay in your own space," and he pulled his arms or legs back in. She tolerated whatever he wanted to do within his own space on his own rug, and he became familiar with his defined area. As children progress through NDD therapy, they usually show naturally improved body awareness and profoundly less flailing about. The defined space also allows those around them to tolerate the flailing until the children are able to define their own space for themselves.

Other children are restless or fidgety. There seems to be a variety of reasons for this. When some highly intelligent children are bored or unchallenged, they become restless, fidgety, or ready to move on. This is because they are intellectually ahead of the discussion or lesson presentation. While some bright students sit and maybe daydream, others become restless. These children make good helpers, or do well when given projects to complete. They tend to easily recognize busy work and may feel insulted if not given something "worthwhile" to do. Restlessness may also be a symptom of neuro-developmental delay. Children with retained primitive reflexes may be uncomfortable in chairs or when standing for very long. Their bodies may not be ready to demonstrate the posture required of them. Some of these children also show auditory processing difficulties and, until they mature within the central nervous system, restless behavior may linger.

Occasionally parents complain that their children cannot sit still; parts of their bodies are constantly moving about. In my office, their feet might be swaying or bouncy, or their hands are playing with an object, buttons, or anything within reach. Others lean against a parent, or try to curl into a parent's lap. Many mothers have said they do not like sitting on the couch to read with their child because the child cannot sit still. I have seen this change in children after they work through stimulation and inhibition of the primitive reflexes, the vestibular system shows stability, and the listening therapy is complete. In my experience, it often requires completion of both NDD therapy and listening therapy before this significantly improves.

Some personality types have high energy. These children perform better when given outlets for physical exertion. Others show an imbalance — they experience sudden and drastic changes in energy levels. I remember one boy in particular who showed an extreme imbalance in energy levels. During our time together, he complained that his arms hurt, he was tired, and he needed to rest. I suggested he lie on the floor, rest, and just talk to me. He lay down and almost immediately jumped back up and started doing jumping jacks. At other moments during the assessment, I paused to write notes (so he could rest) and invariably he jumped up off the floor, danced and then flung himself about. When I asked his parents about his play time at home, they said he often showed low energy and would ride his bicycle for only short periods of time. I witnessed both extremes that day — low and high energy. This boy seemed completely unable to regulate his own energy. As time progressed with his NDD therapy program, he showed more stable energy levels.

Vestibular dysfunction may contribute to hyperactivity. I have seen countless children who appear to be hyperactive, yet when I ask them to stand still without moving, they nearly fall over. As long as they move, they feel balance and control; as soon as movement stops, they lose any sense of balance. So, they keep moving.

Hyperactivity can also be triggered by stimuli. Certain foods such as sugar or food dyes cause hyperactivity in some children. Improper use of asthmatic/respiratory inhalers that mimic adrenaline can cause hyperactivity. Too much screen time, including TV, video games, iPads, etc., can be overstimulating for many children and stir them into hyperactivity. I cannot emphasize enough the dramatic changes I have seen regarding children's hyperactive behavior when their parents reduce or eliminate screen time.

...reduced time in front of a TV or other screens positively and quickly brings improvement in most children.

As children progress through NDD therapy, I often remind parents that the behavior of their children may demonstrate various phases of development for a time. A mother of twin six-year-olds was frustrated because her boys were constantly busy, busy, busy. She used the word "hyper." Together we watched them play, and as soon as we recognized that their behavior at that moment was like that of two-year-olds, the mother was able to relax. She realized she needed to respond to them at the age level they behaved instead of their physiological age; their behaviors varied hour-to-hour and day-to-day. For example, their attention span when looking at books was like that of three-year olds, but it was age appropriate when watching men at work outside a window. Some children may blatantly show behaviors in an age-progressive manner, and others seem to skip about randomly until eventually developmental ages more appropriately line up with physiological ages.

Attention and Concentration

Lack of attention and inability to focus or concentrate can originate from numerous sources. In my experience, reduced time in front of a TV or other screens positively and quickly brings improvement in most children. For others, auditory processing difficulties, vestibular dysfunction, and/or the continued presence of the primitive reflexes contribute to the problem. I have seen some children better able to focus and concentrate when the Moro Reflex (discussed in chapter 3) shows some inhibition because they are less sensitive to and not as easily stimulated by outside influences and distractions. Sounds or movements are not as intense and no longer pull their thoughts away. Sometimes classroom walls are visually overstimulating and, unless some of the wall decorations come down, some children are unable to focus. I have seen classrooms in which there is literally not one area of blank wall space. Something colorful is tacked to every available space in the room. I find it visually distracting to be in a room like that, and I know that many children are highly distracted by it as well.

Lack of structure in a classroom can also contribute

to attention difficulties. Many children with neuro-developmental delay are unable to self-direct (just as toddlers do not self-direct), yet a classroom situation may call for self-direction much of the time. The more structured the classroom environment, the better children seem to perform overall.

Interestingly, some children demonstrate lack of interest or boredom through inattentive behaviors. I know of one middle-school-aged boy who said he talked to others, got too loud, and then got into trouble. I asked him why he started talking to others, and he said he did it when he was bored. Acting out when bored is not a reason I would accept for use of drugs such as Ritalin, yet that is exactly what this boy's school repeatedly suggested. (I was not surprised when the boy acknowledged that the TV was on most of the time at home.)

Some children experience improved ability to focus and stay on task during or after the listening therapy. They are better able to tune out auditory distractions and background noises so they can tune into what needs their attention. Before the listening therapy, all sounds or noises reached their ears equally, and they were unable to separate what to listen to and what to ignore. Several teenagers have described to me the difference they have found after the listening therapy regarding their ability to tune in and tune out sounds appropriately. They typically share they are more able to listen and comprehend lectures or presentations from their teachers and better able to ignore ambient, superfluous sounds.

Play

Signs of neuro-developmental delay often accompany play and social interactions. I hear about children not interacting well with other children. Older children may continue to parallel play like toddlers — play by themselves alongside other children. Sometimes older children still play immaturely with dolls or stuffed animals, or are fascinated by kiddy characters such as Thomas the Train. Some children do not really play with others but seem to dominate or control others. For example, a child may grab a toy out of another's hand because he wants to play with it. This seems incredibly selfish and inappropriate, yet we think nothing of it when a 15- or 18-month-old child does it. I am not surprised to hear about play such as this in an older child undergoing NDD therapy because developmentally that may be the age in which such behavior would be the norm. I expect to hear several months later that these children have begun to play with a little more maturity, which progresses until the style of play becomes more age appropriate. I remember a mother called one day, concerned because her seven-year-old was sitting in the laundry basket tossing the clothes every which way. Yes, that is toddler behavior. Fortunately, it is a passing phase.

> The child needs to know what he does well.

Typically associated with autistic behavior, many children play as though obsessed with a specific toy or group of toys. They cannot think of anything other than their toy airplane, or Legos, or Star Wars collections. Some children obsessively play with one thing, move onto something else, and obsessively play with it until a new toy comes along. Others play with the same thing(s) seemingly forever. Fortunately, as children progress through NDD therapy, this type of play generally matures to more age-appropriate play.

Depression

Unfortunately, symptoms and periods of depression-like behavior are observed in some children during their NDD therapy. For many, it surfaces when they become fully aware of their own inadequacies or they begin to understand the bullying comments from their peers. They realize, perhaps for the first time, that they are different from their peers. In most cases, they not only realize they are different but also that they do not "measure up." This is a painful time for them and painful to watch as well. I encourage parents and teachers to find opportunities to acknowledge and praise successes of the child, whether they are age-appropriate or not. As long as the child does one thing well, that "thing" becomes a focal point for a time. The child needs to know what he does well. Areas in which the child struggles should be placed on the back burner until he begins to feel better about himself and his abilities. I have seen children work through this beautifully when parents and teachers surround them with support, love, and encouragement.

Depression-like moods can be manifested in other ways. I remember meeting a lovely young lady, 11 years old, whose life had gone well until the previous summer when she fell onto a gymnasium floor and suffered a concussion. The concussion healed, but her parents were gravely concerned because their daughter was no longer the same person. Once an outgoing, gregarious person, she had become quiet and reserved. Sitting in noisy rooms or noisy cars annoyed her, and she suffered frequent headaches. She became easily fatigued and was no longer able to keep up her outstanding performance with school work. She sought the quiet of her bedroom for rest. Professionals checked her for depression and migraines, but she did not fit the patterns for either. I agreed to see her as I wondered if perhaps the trauma of her fall and injury might have caused one or more primitive reflexes to resurface. Sure enough, several primitive reflexes were apparent, and her eye movements showed impaired convergence, tracking, and hand-eye tracking. A homeopathic remedy helped her headaches, but the moods and fatigue continued. Through the next several months of NDD therapy, the primitive reflexes withdrew, and her outgoing personality returned. Eye movements were smooth; she returned to working hard at school, and her energy levels came back to what they had been prior to her fall.

A few fortunate families do not encounter notable disturbances in their children's behavior or emotions but, in general, it seems to be par for the course. As the next chapter explains, this is particularly the case for children with a strongly-retained Moro Reflex. I describe to parents that they need to "ride the waves" with their children, and they will reach a time in which the waves rest calmly on a sandy beach. Joy comes to those who ride it out and do not give up.

PART 2:
PRIMITIVE REFLEXES

Chapter 3

Moro Reflex

Nearly 100 percent of children I work with show a continued presence of the infant startle (Moro) reflex. The reflex is easily identified in an infant. When a loud noise, sudden movement, loss of head support, or bright light startles an infant, the Moro Reflex engages. Described in slow motion, the reflex causes the infant to instantly stretch out their arms from a curled-up position. The head and body simultaneously arch backward, the baby takes a deep breath, the arms extend outward, and the hands open. After a brief moment, the head, arms, and legs return toward the body, the arms cross, hands close, and breath is released. This is nearly always accompanied by loud crying. At birth, the Moro Reflex is believed to be an automatic facilitator of a baby's first breath and clearing of the windpipe.

My older daughter delivered her first child at a midwifery center and invited me to attend the birth. While her husband coached her through her labor and supported her during delivery on a birthing stool, I watched this new little grandchild emerge into the world with an immediate Moro Reflex, as expected. Midwives and nurses then helped my daughter onto the adjacent bed and placed her newborn on top of her tummy. My heart overflowed as I stood mesmerized by the movements of this tiny little girl. She lifted her head up off her mommy's tummy, turned it this way and that, lay her head back down, and then up and around again and again. I was astounded by such lively head movements within the first few minutes of birth. No drugs had been involved throughout the labor or delivery and this baby was active, alert, and moving. About an hour later, as she was weighed and measured, she again displayed a Moro Reflex. This is expected in a newborn.

The Moro Reflex should naturally withdraw within the first four months following birth. Some children, however, may become "stuck" in a Moro Reflex before, at, or after birth, or they may not have experienced the developmental stages leading to natural withdrawal of the reflex. Trauma at any age might trigger the Moro Reflex to surface as an involuntary and spontaneous survival mechanism.

In an older child, the Moro Reflex may manifest as "fight or flight" behavior, impulsivity, anger, emotional vulnerability, withdrawal tendencies, rigidity, and/or sensory imbalances. I often see children who can be described as extreme in one or more of these areas. While some are hypersensitive to nearly everything, others might be the opposite. I often see a combination of both. They might be sensitive to sound and cover their ears when a horn honks or when the vacuum cleaner is turned on, but then they turn the volume on the TV so high that it annoys other family members. They may be extremely sensitive to clothes or anything that touches their skin, but then they might brush off a major crash from their bike or scooter. Emotions are frequently extremely high. Some children, on the other hand, are severely withdrawn so that one wonders if they might crawl inside themselves and disappear. In my experience, sensory disorders have been consistently connected with retention of the Moro Reflex.

The process of stimulating the Moro Reflex into withdrawal may take considerable time. I have never seen it withdraw in less than six months. In most cases, it has taken about a year. I believe the Moro Reflex is slow to inhibit because it can profoundly influence overall functioning of a child's body. The sensory system (sound, light, taste, touch, texture) is affected by the reflex and so are emotions. The child has a lot to work through, and it does not happen overnight. Some children work it through slowly and evidence is seen in one area at a time; others seem to work through areas like the peeling of an onion — in layers. I have witnessed this type of progress in many children. Evidence of withdrawal of the Moro Reflex shows in one area and then another and another, and then all of a sudden, the child is working through the first area again but in a deeper way. The process is always observable emotionally, behaviorally, and/or physiologically.

Because the Moro Reflex affects emotions so profoundly, I make it a practice to forewarn parents they may initially experience a bumpy ride in their home for a while. A child's emotions may be a rollercoaster while this reflex is undergoing withdrawal; they may undergo a chronological series of emotions such as crying easily for a time, followed by being overly excitable, followed by incredible anger. It is different for every child. When I first meet with parents, prior to starting NDD therapy, I often hear, "Well, we know it cannot get any worse than it already is." It often does get worse for a time. The exercises for the Moro Reflex vary per child and are monitored carefully. Too much stimulation might send a child "up the wall." The goal is to carefully stimulate the brain stem so that changes are subtle and as smooth as possible for the child. I encourage parents to do the assigned exercise with only the child enrolled in NDD therapy and not attempt to do it with siblings, neighbors, friends, or relatives. The exercise movements are very stimulating, whether or not it appears that way, and have a definite effect on one's emotions. They frequently require a parent to move the child in a specific manner.

> The goal is to carefully stimulate the brain stem so that changes are subtle and as smooth as possible for the child.

Some children are instantly tired and ready to go to sleep. Others immediately show infantile body positions or movements. Right after an exercise, it is not unusual to see fetal positions or cocooning of some sort. It may look as if the child is simulating a womb-like position. Mothers who have had experience in occupational therapy, nursing, or physical therapy are quick to recognize infantile positions following an exercise. I remember one boy, age seven, cocooned for a short time after his first experience with his exercise. While still cocooned but having pulled his head out of the blanket, he scooted around on the floor on his back, rolled over onto his tummy and then again onto his back so that he lay at my feet. I looked down, and he started playing peek-a-boo with me just like my then 15-month-old granddaughter. Babyish, infantile behavior is typical in the beginning. I have also seen children demonstrate irregular breathing during an exercise or awkward movements of the mouth, face, head, or body. Some break out into a sweat that immediately stops once the exercise is over. Sometimes I hear the tummy growling throughout the exercise, or a child passes gas continually until the exercise is finished. Reactions of some sort are a common occurrence initially and should be expected.

Behavior and emotions as described in the previous chapter are most extreme when a strong Moro Reflex is present. The following sections describe common observations of children's experiences as they undergo exercises that target inhibition of the Moro Reflex. Every child works through NDD therapy in his and her own manner, and observations usually prove to be signs of measurable changes and withdrawal of one or more of the primitive reflexes.

Breathing

Breathing irregularities are not unusual when a child shows a continued presence of the Moro Reflex. Newborns naturally breathe irregularly for a time, and some children seem to continue in this mode well beyond infancy. I frequently see it in older children and teens, particularly as an outward sign of stress, embarrassment, uncertainty, or of something requiring intense concentration. Some hold their breath when they stand and turn their head in any direction. When some children tip their heads back or when they close their eyes, breathing changes. Others stop breathing when their body turns in a specific way. I have been surprised at how many hold their breath when they write or draw. They hold their breath while writing and then take a new breath between sentences, or they hold their breath while drawing and inhale between each drawn shape. This can cause tremendous fatigue, and may interfere with a child's academic performance. This usually settles down and breathing becomes more regular as children continue with NDD therapy.

Sleeping

Parents recurrently notice changes in their children's sleeping patterns. While some children begin to sleep 12 or 13 hours per night, others experience a period in which sleep is difficult. Some children show the need for an afternoon nap. I have worked with many children who would function better if their school day was shortened until they matured enough to handle a full day of school. Others go through a phase of waking up during the night and in need of a parent's comfort. It is not unusual to hear that a child desires to sleep with Mom and Dad again.

Some children experience a period of vivid, highly detailed dreams and/or nightmares. As the primitive reflexes work toward inhibition, it is expected that the visual system will be affected, which sometimes manifests through dreaming. Some children start dreaming for the first time, and others start remembering their dreams. Dreams commonly become detailed, colorful, and intense. A few children experience a brief period of night terrors. I also hear that some children no longer need a hall light, or night light; some children decide they want to try sleeping with their bedroom door closed, and it proves successful. Others, who used to struggle immensely with being able to get to sleep, find that they more easily fall asleep, and they sleep more soundly. Some children who regularly talk in their sleep or sleepwalk usually stop at some point during the therapy. My own daughter walked the house during the night, and it did not stop until she was nearly finished with NDD therapy. Changes in sleep vary; they can be almost rollercoaster-like for a while. In time, sleep should settle to more normal patterns. Remember, infants and often toddlers do the same in normal development. This commonly fluctuates for a while during NDD therapy.

Bedwetting

Numerous children, many in their teens, have bedwetting issues. I have seen interesting yet inconsistent changes so that I am unable point my finger at any one cause. I do believe it is related to the vestibular system and directly associated with the vagus nerve, a nerve that is rooted in the brain stem and reaches to all the major organs of the body. Some children instantly stop bedwetting from just one exercise (it is not the same exercise for each child – what works for one does not work for another). Some children stop bedwetting when they complete the sound therapy program. Others stop bedwetting when the Spinal Galant Reflex (discussed in Chapter 5) has inhibited. Some children have constipation issues, which have to be addressed before bedwetting ceases. Others have stopped when they tried specific oils or a homeopathic remedy. Again, it seems to be different with each child.

Eating

Eating habits typically change as well. I often hear that a child who initially was a very picky eater starts volunteering to try new foods. Some children find textures that once bothered them no longer do. Others like the taste of things they once disliked and sometimes dislike tastes they once liked. Overall, eating improves even though it can be up and down for a while. Many eating and chewing issues may also relate to the presence of a Rooting Reflex (discussed in Chapter 5). I remember one family in particular who found that their child ate better when fed baby food for a short time. The child started on finger food a short time later and then an interest in eating foods with utensils developed.

Stimming

Children initially labeled as autistic often engage in stimming (repetitive movements that are self-stimulating), such as flapping the hands or arms, stroking an object over and over, or repeating a particular sound. They often stim when they are overstimulated in one or more of the senses. I have worked with children who initially stimmed when the barometric pressure changed. (Some children's moods also change based on the barometric pressure or when exposed to strong winds.) Interestingly, infants flap their arms when they are excited, such as when they eagerly await their mothers' preparation for breastfeeding. We think nothing of an infant "stimming," but we naturally become concerned when an older child does it. Consistently, children with neuro-developmental delay beginning at the brain stem level often manifest behaviors of a much younger child. Instead of helping the child recapture earlier stages of development, our culture tends to label them and tries to "teach" them age-appropriate behaviors.

I remember a 10-year-old boy who walked and ran in circles while holding his toy shark in the air as if it were flying. His parents and teachers were all concerned. I saw it as early-childhood play — imaginary play with a toy. As he progressed through NDD therapy, his play matured and walking/running in a circle with his shark stopped on its own. Other children who demonstrated stimming behavior prior to NDD therapy have shown gradually increased maturity until the behavior has ceased altogether or occurs only in situations in which they are significantly overstimulated.

TV and screens are overstimulating for many people. I remember a mother whose son stimmed only while watching TV. Instead of turning off the TV, she wanted his behavior to change. Another boy stimmed almost nonstop. His parents and grandparents agreed to curb his screen time and the stimming drastically reduced. The next primary complaint became his mode of play, which consisted of repeating verbatim cartoons or movies as if in an imaginary world. As screen time was eliminated, the boy became more and more connected to the real world, and his repetitive cartoon conversations stopped. Overstimulation from screens is not atypical or abnormal. The fine print in video game literature warns about the possibility of seizures in some people. If video games might cause something as extreme as seizures in some children, the potential for other problems related to overstimulation should also be cause for concern.

Sensory Imbalances

Sensory integration disorder (also called sensory processing disorder) is a widespread diagnosis. As we think of normal development, newborns and young infants do not maturely respond to sensory input. They react with cries to express their every need. They should, however, naturally begin to process sensory input appropriately through natural growth. Sounds, bright lights or sudden movement may initially trigger a startle response, but as the child grows, more natural responses are observed. Most children naturally experience sensitivities to taste or textures when first learning to eat. We expect infants and young toddlers to express behavioral reactions (instead of thought-out responses) that improve through maturity and growth. The sensory system gradually, over time, is able to make more appropriate motor and behavioral responses. The central nervous system matures through normal development so that sensory input is received with more appropriate responses.

Older children who show the continued presence of primitive reflexes may continue to struggle with inadequate responses to sensory input. I have met many children who at first cannot go to movie theaters (the screen is over stimulating or the sounds are too loud), or have to leave their church services until the instruments stop playing because the music is too loud. Some children cannot tolerate noisy crowds, sirens, school fire alarms, bright lights, fluorescent lights, or textures in foods or clothes. I have met children who refuse to remove their socks and others who refuse to wear socks. I have met countless children who refuse to wear blue jeans because the pants are too confining at the waistline. They need loose-fitting, elastic waistbands.

Another common observation in children who show the continued presence of the Moro Reflex is poor eye contact. Although it is often considered symptomatic of autism, I have not seen this to be the case. Newborns do not have eye contact. It is part of natural development. Therefore, it should be considered an indicator of neuro-developmental delay. In normal development, eye contact develops as the Moro Reflex withdraws. In my experience, children naturally develop eye contact as they particularly work through the Moro Reflex.

Although some children with poor eye contact have dilated pupils, other children show good eye contact but dilated, contracted, or unresponsive pupils. Once in a while, parents notice increased dilation in the first few months of NDD therapy. Typically, more normal and natural reactions to light are observed in a child's pupils within a short time.

As children progress through NDD therapy, interesting sensory responses are often noted. I share with parents that they may find that their child experiences a period in which one sensory system may be hypersensitive, followed by another and then another. Or, children may experience sudden hypersensitivity in all the senses at one time. Sensitivities typically increase before they decrease. I remember a young girl whose mother said that one Sunday afternoon at a restaurant the girl nearly had a meltdown because all of a sudden the sounds and lighting overwhelmed her, and then the taste of her food, which she usually liked, was "too much." The very next day, the agitations seemed to have disappeared and never returned. Normally, I hear about this over a period of time, not in one afternoon.

Some children seem more agitated and irritable for a time. Parents might feel like they are hanging by a thread as they attempt to cope with their child's agitated state. Invariably, when I retest these children, I find they are working through multiple primitive reflexes all at one time. A child's moods are affected when multiple changes occur simultaneously within the central nervous system.

As children participate in their daily exercise, they sometimes have physical complaints, or their parents notice reactions in their bodies. Children may complain that their eyes, heads, necks, or tummies itch. When I hear the eyes are itchy I know the next time I check oculo-motor movements, I can expect to see improvements. Commonly, I observe the pupils are responding more appropriately to light. Parents may notice strange mouth or facial movements, yawns, sneezes, head bobbing, etc. Experience has shown that all these reactions are indicative of changes taking place in the central nervous system, leading to withdrawal of the primitive reflexes.

I expect to hear at some point during NDD therapy that these children are now able to attend a movie at a theater and enjoy it, or the musical instruments in the church services are no longer overwhelming, or blue jeans are now comfortable. The sensory system gradually shows assimilation.

More recently parents have described their children as "sensory seeking" (getting satisfaction from stimulating one's senses). This may very well be symptomatic of neuro-developmental delay, but when I hear about it as a child nears the end of his or her therapy program, I have found it to be misunderstood situations. Parents are accustomed to specific behaviors in their children; as changes come through NDD therapy, their children behave differently. Misinterpretation of behaviors occurs when parents base new behaviors on previous difficulties. For many of these parents, once a child shows maturity at the brain stem level, the sensory system functions

> Misinterpretation of behaviors occurs when parents base new behaviors on previous difficulties.

more normally; normal play or personal preferences

might be misinterpreted. I remember a family came to my office one day and described wonderful progress with their son but then expressed concern about what they described as "sensory seeking" behavior. While we talked, the boy played on the mat in my office, busy with somersaults, cartwheels, dance moves, karate-type moves, etc. The parents said he had started doing this recently, and they were concerned. What I saw was a boy who had become fully aware of his own body. He was finally able to play with balance and motor movements; he was able to perform specific and precise movements with his body that were age appropriate. This was not sensory seeking behavior. This was a boy fully in control of his own body and enjoying it!

Another mother described her daughter as recently showing "sensory seeking" behavior at the same time she completed NDD therapy. When I asked for an example, she said it was evident in only one area — the daughter refused to wear pants made with spandex. She preferred looser-fitting pants such as jeans. This was not sensory seeking behavior. This was a case of personal preference. Some people prefer natural fabrics, and others like synthetics; some like loose, comfortable clothes; others are comfortable in tight but stretchy fabrics. One preference over another does not suggest sensory dysfunction. We can easily become overly critical and forget what "normal" is.

Self-Awareness

Numerous parents describe their children as clueless to their surroundings or completely unaware of how different they are from their peers. Children in school may not realize they are several grades below their peers or that anything about them is not as it should be. I meet a lot of children who are happy in their little worlds, love their teachers, and are generally merry about life, completely unaware that they function under par.

In cases like this, I forewarn parents that I expect these children to reach a point during NDD therapy in which they become fully aware of just how different things are, and it may stir their emotions and behavior. Sometimes parents describe a new behavior in which their child shows embarrassment about his or her own inadequacies because he or she has become aware of it for the first time. As parents carefully describe it to me in the presence of their child, the child shows embarrassment from hearing his or her parents talk about their social or academic situations. The awareness has become evident.

On the other hand, some children, especially teenagers, are fully aware of how they "do not fit" with their peers before we ever start NDD therapy. Whether or not the individual is aware of it from the beginning or becomes aware of it later, careful attention is required. When a child becomes fully aware that she is unlike her peers, she may appear to withdraw or show signs of depression. This becomes a critical time and calls for direct attention. I encourage parents and teachers to pull back on demands and start emphasizing and focusing on things for which praise can be expressed. The child needs to hear and experience success and worth. If academics are hard, this is not the time to push. If the child is shy, this is not the time to push peer interaction and social skills. This is the time to think about what the child can do well. The child needs to engage in activities and opportunities that allow her to feel good about what she can do. Each time I have witnessed this phase, it passes, but it should be recognized as an important phase of development. Normal patterns of development provide individuals with the ability to discern how well they blend with their peers.

This rough period is hardest on children who attend school away from home. Our children's peers are not as kind as we would like, so support and encouragement usually have to come from home. I have often requested that parents talk to their children's teachers, especially at this point, so that encouragement and support will hopefully come from the school as well as from home. Because of potentially fewer opportunities for unkind behavior from peers, homeschoolers typically pass through this phase more smoothly, some so subtly the parents are barely aware of it.

Memory

Memory, like other areas, does not improve in the same manner with every child. Some children struggle with it for quite some time; others suddenly show remarkable memory. Parents have shared about their adopted children starting to remember their pasts and beginning to tell about experiences from previous foster homes or orphanages. Some children show better recall of events from their earlier years or the previous week or previous day. Parents have shared their surprise when their child remembered a specific event or occasion from the past. With this, I often see children better able to separate one day from another. Next, I look for the ability to separate days, weeks and seasons. Little children start to remember how to spell their names; older children are better able to tell me what they did that morning or the day before. Some children are able to put events into order for the first time and tell me what they did first, next and so forth. Many show better day-to-day learning; what used to get lost from one day to the next starts to improve, and repetitive learning is less frequent. I remember a mother sharing that after the first two months of NDD therapy, her 11-year-old daughter started the school year (homeschooling). She was ecstatic because her daughter retained what she had learned from the previous school year (it had been the same thing year after year). For the first time ever, she was able to move forward academically.

As children near completion of NDD therapy, parents sometimes struggle with grasping whether or not memory continues to be a problem. I remember a boy whose mother said he continued to struggle with remembering what he had learned from one day to the next long after it should no longer have been a problem. I met with the boy for a reading and writing lesson and discovered that his problem was not memory; he was focused on trying to jump ahead. When we talked about staying with me, he complied and easily retained the lesson. Another mother said her son, having completed NDD therapy, was not able to remember instructions as well as he should have based on his developmental age. After spending some time with the boy, I learned that he was easily able to remember instructions; the problem was he stubbornly chose to follow his own ideas about the way things should be done. What once were memory problems became expressions of personality.

As the Moro Reflex inhibits and maturity comes, children's personalities become more distinct, and parents are better able to see who their children are. I remind parents that we cannot change innate character, but we will be able to see it more clearly. Children move from the place in which allowances must be made to a place in which they are capable of making choices and able to be held responsible for their choices. This is when parents have to change with their children and begin to hold their children accountable. The allowances once made no longer apply.

> Children move from the place in which allowances must be made to a place in which they are capable of making choices and able to be held responsible for their choices.

Chapter 4

Tonic Labyrinthine Reflex

The Tonic Labyrinthine Reflex (TLR) is closely related to the Moro reflex in the first few months of life, as both reflexes are activated by movement of the head. When an adult lays a baby across her arm and tucks the baby's head forward, the baby goes into a fetal position. When the baby's head falls below spine level, the body pushes up and out so that the torso extends as well.[2]

The Tonic Labyrinthine Reflex (TLR) typically emerges at birth. The head-forward expression of the reflex (flexion) usually withdraws at about four months of age and the head-backward component (extension), when the head falls below spine level, begins withdrawal six weeks after birth and may not fully inhibit until about age three. As this reflex withdraws in normal development, a child becomes able to control head movements voluntarily, creeping and crawling mature, balance and muscle tone develop, visual processing develops, and depth perception begins.

Infants and toddlers generally work through this reflex in observable stages. They first develop the ability to lift their heads up off the floor when lying on their tummies. (I have observed nearly year-old toddlers unable to creep or crawl because continuation of this reflex has prevented them from lifting their heads up off the floor.) An infant of about six months of age who is first learning to sit on his or her own may frequently show balance difficulties when the head moves in different positions. As the child matures and becomes more familiar and comfortable with sitting on his or her own, balance remains steady regardless of head position. A toddler, in time, is able to move his or her head while standing without having it affect balance. Toddlers' standing balance also matures in a progressive manner. They initially curl and grip with their toes and frequently rock back onto their heels. At first, they routinely fall, but, as balance becomes more manageable, they are able to rock back onto their heels and then flatten their feet again while maintaining balance. I see this same occurrence in countless older children for whom balance remains difficult. Either they curl and grip their toes as they attempt to maintain standing balance, or they repeatedly rock back onto their heels.

I remember watching my 20-month-old granddaughter stand in the middle of a room. Her balance was strong and stable for her age, and she was able to maintain balance while moving her head into different positions. One day I studied her movements as she tipped her head back to watch the spinning ceiling fan. She then turned her head to the side, looked at the switch on the wall, and then tipped her head back toward the ceiling fan again. The first time she tipped her head back, her shoulders lifted slightly. The second time, no body movements engaged and her balance remained steady and strong. Many older children whose TLR has not fully withdrawn are not able to do those same movements comfortably.

The following areas are typically troublesome for children with a retained TLR and show great improvement when this reflex has inhibited.

Head Flexion and Extension

Some children appear to be overly floppy with low tone; other children are rigid and stiff. A child may have low tone or be stiff and rigid due to retention of both the Moro and the TLR. The body, legs, or torso want to reflexively respond and move as one with the head instead of allowing separate head movement. This leads to either floppy movements or rigid tightening of the muscles. Until head movements comfortably engage independently of body movements, children may show abnormal tone. I often describe normal head movement as similar to a ketchup bottle — the lid flips back and then comes forward and closes, yet the bottle does not move. When one's head moves backward (extension) or forward (flexion), the body should be able to remain still without extraneous movements or loss of balance. Some children cannot maintain smooth forward and backward head movements, while others struggle with it in just one direction.

Children with a strong TLR may strain profoundly with normal day-to-day activities. Some become dizzy or lightheaded from forward/backward head movements, and others lose their balance when their head moves into flexion or extension. For many, breathing changes when head position changes — it may become irregular, or children may hold their breath until their head position returns to center, facing forward. I commonly find that when children struggle profoundly with head flexion/extension they also suffer from motion sickness, particularly sharp stops in which their head may be thrown forward. When I encounter a child with a strongly retained TLR in extension, I encourage the parents to avoid requiring their child to hold that position for a time, as it may possibly trigger negative behavior, fear, exasperation, lack of eye contact, or even a Moro Reflex. For example, if a child needs a scolding, it would be better for the parent to lower him or herself to the child's eye level before demanding eye contact and delivering a scolding (instead of telling the child to look up — tip the head backward — and make eye contact). Many of these children are not comfortable with tipping their heads backward until this reflex has withdrawn. Requiring this position from such a child may trigger emotional outbursts.

Another common occurrence I have heard about is when a child is asked to tip his head back at the dentist's office. Parents who have shared with their dentists that their children are not comfortable with head extension have received overwhelming support from their dentists. The children typically get through their visits more smoothly without having to move their heads in positions which are still uncomfortable for them. As this reflex begins to withdraw, children no longer struggle with head extension. Parents have shared delightful stories about their children tipping their heads back to look at cloud formations, planes flying overhead, or floating balloons. These become new experiences as children show withdrawal of the Tonic Labyrinthine Reflex.

Eye Movements

As the TLR withdraws, I also normally see dramatic improvement in eye movements. My daughter initially struggled overwhelmingly with depth perception and visual figure-ground. Visual figure-ground requires the ability to see a detailed object within a busy background (children like to do this with *Where's Waldo* books). I remember a time when our family visited castle remains and I coerced my daughter into climbing a wrought-iron circular stairway with me. She nearly had a panic attack before we were halfway up the stairway. I had to back her down again, squeezing past the line of people that had been following us. As my daughter recovered, she explained that each time she placed her foot on a step, she could see through to the ground and was unable to tell where her foot would land — on a step, or all the way down onto the dirt below. Visual information was inaccurate — what she knew to be true did not match what her eyes were telling her. This experience was a frightening eye-opener for me about how complicated these problems can be and how unbearable it must be to live with them. Fortunately, this is no longer a problem for my daughter.

> Visual information was inaccurate — what she knew to be true did not match what her eyes were telling her.

Eye convergence (when both eyes draw inward as a team to focus on an object) often improves when the Tonic Labyrinthine Reflex withdraws. Some children's coloring suddenly improves and they are able to color within the lines, or an interest in drawing begins, or more detailed drawings can be observed. Hobbies and interests that demand close-up work may surface. Another obvious sign would be a new interest, desire, or motivation for reading. When parents have suddenly noticed their children reading comic books or labels on containers, I immediately check for measurable changes, particularly regarding this reflex. I have met children who previously read with one eye. As the Tonic Labyrinthine Reflex withdrew, they started reading with both eyes. Some children automatically begin to read, or reading improves, or an interest in reading develops. Such is not always the case, however. Older children often require quality tutoring so that they "unlearn" poor, compensatory reading habits.

In my experience, expecting children to read despite these retained reflexes and the resultant inadequate eye movements requires them to find compensatory methods and assume poor habits. The habits later have to be "unlearned" so that good reading develops. On the other hand, parents who wait until their children are physiologically ready to read usually see better and faster results. It is not unusual for me to hear that within a year or two after completing NDD therapy (and for some, after completing the listening therapy) a child has become one of the top readers in his class. Or, I hear that a child progressed from reading at first- or second-grade level to sixth-grade level or higher within a few months to a year. Yet some continue to struggle, confused because the school teaches reading one way while *Anna's House* or parents teach a different way. These children tend to make considerable progress during the summer months when school is out and only one teaching method is employed.

Balance and Body Awareness

After birth, children show development progressing from the head to the feet; awareness and control of the extremities develops downward through the body. They learn to use their arms and hands before their legs and feet. Older children who show delay in development often continue to struggle with full awareness and/or control of their extremities. During an initial assessment, I commonly find that a child's ability to recognize points of touch on their extremities is impaired. Many children are not able to match points of touch particularly on the lower arms and/or lower legs. This changes during NDD therapy. As the Moro and Tonic Labyrinthine reflexes withdraw, I typically find that children are better able to recognize points of touch all over their limbs, and improved awareness of their bodies in space becomes evident as well.

Children's complaints often reveal specific reflexes that are in the process of withdrawal. During one particular NDD exercise, children commonly complain that one or both arms or shoulders ache. Within a short time, the complaint disappears and I find that the Tonic Labyrinthine Reflex shows at least some inhibition. I remember during one checkup visit, a mother commented as a side note that her son complained one night after his exercise that his lower legs and feet felt like pins were sticking them. I retested the boy's reflexes and ability to recognize touch. The Moro and Tonic Labyrinthine reflexes showed significant inhibition. Just a few months prior, he had been unable to match touches to his lower legs to within three inches. The retest showed precise matches with only slight misses on the inside of one calf. It was as if this boy's awareness of his lower legs and feet had awakened. Other children often comment about feeling tingles on their tummies or in their fingertips. Tingling, itches, or unusual sensations typically cease after a short period of time.

Within the first several months of an individual's NDD therapy, changes in balance and body awareness are usually observed. Most children initially show poor balance or difficulties with static (without movement such as when standing still) or dynamic (during movement such as when riding a bicycle) balance. Many parents share that within about the first three to four months of NDD therapy their children seem to be more active and busy, almost hyper. As parents and I continue discussion during a family's office visit, I observe the child out of the corner of my eye. I regularly see improvements in body awareness as children engage in activities that require balance — handstands, somersaults, cart wheels, dance movements, martial arts poses, jumping off of objects, etc. Some children come into my office anxious to show me that they can stand on their heads, or they ask me to help them as they position into a handstand. These are fun and exciting moments. Instead of flailing about, the child shows organized, purposeful movements typically related to balance. I often hear about children being able to float on water for the first time, or about more fluid movements in daily activities such as bike riding, skateboarding, or skiing. Jumping off of objects may indicate the child is developing an improved sense of depth perception as well as body awareness. The overall desire for physical activities commonly increases.

I remember during a family's office visit, their

seven-year-old-girl placed her head on the floor, her hands near her head with elbows bent, her feet flat against the floor and her bottom in the air. (This is a flexion position of the Symmetrical Tonic Neck Reflex, discussed in Chapter 7, typical of a very young child.) I encouraged her parents to watch for ongoing play and experimentation with balance positions and movements. Later that same day, I was invited to dinner with the family. After dinner, the girl stood behind her mother's chair and pulled herself up into the air by placing one hand on the back of her mother's chair and the other on the back of a chair at the next (empty) table so that her feet were suspended and her arms and body were straight. After her parents got her seated again, we talked about how she had been playing with balance.

Her mother suddenly remembered that just in the last week or two her daughter had been doing the same thing in their kitchen using the handle of the refrigerator door and the counter top. This is an example of typical behavior as balance and body awareness develop, regardless of one's age. My daughter, nearly out of her teens, started dancing around the kitchen and saying, "Look at me," as she balanced on one foot with her arms extended into the air like a ballerina.

> It must be remembered that in normal development the Tonic Labyrinthine Reflex begins withdrawal prior to a child learning to sit for the first time.

As the Tonic Labyrinthine Reflex withdraws, many children do not yet show good posture while seated or standing, and academics may not show much improvement. These things are yet to come. It must be remembered that in normal development the Tonic

Labyrinthine Reflex begins withdrawal prior to a child learning to sit for the first time. The shoulders may still be rounded, and overall postural strength while seated might still be lacking. I have noticed some children become better able to hold their heads erect. In normal development, this is when a child should be having a lot of "tummy time," when the body is first learning to defy the pull of gravity. Inhibition of the TLR is related to development of space perception, depth perception, balance, body awareness, and needed sensory stimulation.

I am often able to understand where a child is in the scheme of things regarding NDD therapy because parents' concerns change. While they may have initially been highly concerned about emotions and behavior, parents later express concerns about postural positions and/or academics. It is often too soon. Progress is coming, but just as a toddler is not expected to read or know her multiplication tables, these children are not quite developmentally ready for higher expectations. Academics commonly remain on the back burner for a bit longer, and seated positions on chairs at desks and tables are still uncomfortable for many children.

One seven-year-old girl I worked with behaved developmentally as a three-year-old in many areas. When she first started NDD therapy, she was not "in this world." She did not make eye contact, did not respond when spoken to, and rarely uttered a word. As the primitive reflexes began to withdraw, she joined this world. Eye contact became apparent, she responded when addressed, and she initiated conversation. A short time later, her mother discussed her child's readiness for accountability as a three-year old (even though she was seven). I held out an empty basket, and as I named one stuffed animal at a time, the girl picked each one up and put it in the basket. She then was expected to say "goodbye" when she left, and she did! She had achieved tremendous gains and required expectations increased as her developmental age increased. Academics remained in the background a bit longer.

NDD therapy and withdrawal of the primitive reflexes is a strategic, progressive process based on normal development. I often remind parents that we have made progress, yet we cannot raise expectations before a child is ready. More is yet to come. Parents who know me are familiar with my saying, "We are not there yet. We will be concerned about that later." I am following the normal pattern of development and watching for what the child will reveal next. Expectations are raised when the child demonstrates he or she is ready. Many parents fear that it might never come. As long as parents hang in there and stay the course, we see progress.

Older children may show withdrawal of the Moro and TLR through NDD therapy at about the same time, or it may occur with one slightly following the other. Either way, by the time both reflexes show inhibition, I expect to see some settling in behavior and emotions, improvement in balance, smoother eye movements, and increased body awareness.

Chapter 5

Rooting, Palmar, Plantar, and Spinal Galant Reflexes

In my experience, when a child shows one or more of the Rooting, Palmar, Plantar, and Spinal Galant reflexes, he or she also usually shows evidence of a Moro Reflex. As the Moro Reflex withdraws, I generally observe that these reflexes withdraw at about the same time. Interestingly, they often withdraw when children engage in specific exercises that target the Moro Reflex instead of specific exercises for each individual reflex. Occasionally I have implemented exercises for one or more of the individual reflexes, such as when I observe withdrawal of the Moro Reflex but one or more of the Rooting, Palmar, Plantar, or Spinal Galant Reflexes has shown little or no withdrawal. Because they most commonly withdraw at about the same time and generally without specific stimulation, I have grouped them together in this chapter.

Rooting Reflex

The Rooting Reflex emerges in the womb and should withdraw when an infant is three to four months of age. A stroke along either side of an infant's mouth produces a turning of the head and causes the mouth to form a ready-to-suck position. It is an automatic, involuntary reflex. While it may be hard to imagine an older child with a continued Rooting Reflex, it is a common occurrence. Children who show an uninhibited Rooting Reflex may have difficulty swallowing bites of food; they may suck on toys, their shirts, pencils, toys, or anything they pick up.

Some children seem not quite ready to chew, especially meats. They prefer liquids or soft foods. As the reflex withdraws, chewing improves, and usually an interest in a greater variety of foods improves as well. I have come to expect fluctuations in eating, food cravings, and food aversions during NDD therapy. As the primitive reflexes withdraw, I usually hear that overall eating is better including a broadening interest in foods.

Eating itself varies among children with the Rooting Reflex. Some may prefer finger food, or they might use their fingers whether or not they are given finger food. Others eat bigger portions with less "playing at the table" if Mom or Dad feeds them for a time, just like with a toddler. Many parents share that, in time, their children's eating shows increased maturity.

I remember one eight-year-old who still used a pacifier. Nothing stopped her frequent use or desire for the pacifier. As she and her mother remained consistent with NDD therapy, the girl stopped using the pacifier on her own accord and her eight-year habit was gone in less than six weeks. This particular case, however, was unusually quick. Other children take much longer to reach the same goal. I often hear, nonetheless, that excessive sucking and chewing on objects decreases or dissipates in time.

Palmar Reflex

The Palmar and Rooting reflexes are closely related in early development and should withdraw within a month or two of each other. When one places a finger or similar object into an infant's palm, the tiny fingers close around the object and grasp tightly. This is the Palmer Reflex in action. Typically, newborns curl their fingers almost into fists. As they breastfeed, their fingers loosen so that as they become full and satisfied, their hands open and their fingers relax. Mouth and hands coordinate concurrently. This correlation can be observed in older children with retained reflexes, particularly when they engage in activities such as eating, writing, or drawing. The mouth moves when the fingers grasp.

Children with the Rooting and/or Palmar reflexes may not want to hold silverware for long while eating, or flat out refuse to hold a spoon or fork. They may prefer to eat finger food, or they may start out using a utensil and as their hunger becomes satisfied they no longer want to hold it. Sometimes these children do not get enough to eat because they may physically fatigue before they have filled their stomachs.

Many children move their lips, mouth, or tongue while their hand grips an object for writing or drawing. As the fingers curl around a pencil, crayon, or marker, the mouth opens and the lips move, or the tongue protrudes. Pencil grip is typically immature when the Palmar Reflex is retained. Many parents tell me their children's special education teachers have them practice pencil grip and/or writing exercises regularly. I say just the opposite. It is not necessarily a special gripper pencil or practice that improves writing. Poor handwriting may be partly due to a continued Palmar Reflex, but it may also include the continued presence of an Asymmetrical Tonic Neck Reflex and/or Symmetrical Tonic Neck Reflex (discussed in chapters 6 and 7). Nevertheless, I usually encourage parents to put writing on the back burner for a time and introduce it when one or more of these reflexes have withdrawn to some extent.

> Poor handwriting may be partly due to a continued Palmar Reflex, but it may also include the continued presence of an Asymmetrical Tonic Neck Reflex and/or Symmetrical Tonic Neck Reflex.

When a child shows appropriate maturity for handwriting, I frequently find that retracing the steps of early writing is most beneficial. I habitually suggest that these children start writing with "fat" utensils, such as fat, bullet-point markers. Parents and teachers usually provide three-year-olds with fat crayons and fat markers to start writing so that they gradually become comfortable with pencil grip. Older children often need to retrace this phase of development for a time. Using a white board allows them to easily erase and does not require precise letter or word spacing. Eye convergence and eye tracking may need to improve, as well as the Asymmetrical Tonic Neck Reflex, before a lot of improvement in writing can be expected. I do not expect good letter or word spacing until the Asymmetrical Tonic Neck Reflex shows some withdrawal. In the meantime, pencil grip can begin if the Palmar Reflex shows some inhibition. Once a child is comfortable with a fat marker, I change to a thin marker. When the child shows comfortable posture and a nice grip with neat handwriting, then I give her a fat pencil, and finally a regular pencil. Lined paper should be modified when the Asymmetrical Tonic Neck Reflex shows some inhibition. Having shared this with a few teachers, they applied this procedure (retracing early development with pencil grip) and were thrilled with the progress they observed.

Plantar Reflex

A Plantar Reflex in the feet is similar to the Palmar Reflex in the hands. Pressure to the ball of the foot causes the toes to reflexively curl. This reflex emerges in utero and typically withdraws at seven to nine months of age. Toddlers generally interchange use of their feet when standing and walking — they may periodically stand with curled or gripping toes and may also walk on their toes or on their heels. This is common through about age three. At times, toddlers' toes curl, making it difficult to put on their shoes. These are early developmental phases and should not be evident in an older child.

When children show a retained Plantar Reflex, their calf muscles remain tight and in a contracted state. Tight calf muscles, in turn, may greatly impact circulation and blood flow throughout the body. Specific muscles in each calf work as a pump to send blood back up to the heart. The body, therefore, relies on muscles in the calves to continually contract and stretch. I work with many children with this reflex whose calf muscles are extremely tight. In these cases, stretching becomes part of the protocol once the reflex withdraws.

Signs of a continued Plantar Reflex in an older child, therefore, include curling the toes, gripping the floor, or walking on the toes. Children may curl or grip their toes when walking, putting on shoes, or striving to maintain balance. I work with many toe walkers who have shown a retained Plantar Reflex. Some professionals describe toe walking as one of many symptoms in the autistic spectrum. I disagree. Every toe walker I have met has shown a continued Plantar Reflex, and the overwhelming majority have never been diagnosed in the autistic spectrum.

On one occasion, an eight-year-old boy's mother expressed that their pediatrician had referred their son for surgery in hopes of correcting his toe walking. I encouraged the mother to call the pediatrician and suggest that perhaps the boy had a continued Plantar Reflex. After doing so, the surgery was cancelled and other possibilities were considered. One 17-year-old toe walker I met had already undergone two surgeries on one foot and one on the other foot in efforts to correct toe walking, yet he continued to walk on his toes.

After inhibition of the Plantar Reflex through NDD therapy, some children have to break the habit of toe walking by conscious effort. Others seem to automatically convert to a natural pattern of walking. A few children have had to wear a brace for a time and others have had to progress through other reflexes before improvements were observed.

> After inhibition of the Plantar Reflex through NDD therapy, some children have to break the habit of toe walking by conscious effort.

I remember working with one 16-year-old who showed slight neuro-developmental delay and was a toe walker. His father, a high school track coach, desperately wanted to find a way to correct it. As the young man worked through NDD therapy, the Plantar Reflex withdrew, yet he continued to walk on his toes. I suggested that it had become habitual. The teen's father then insisted that his son walk up and down the long street in front of their house every day after school using slow, deliberate, heel-to-toe technique. When the young man comfortably walked heel-to-toe, his father insisted he start running up and down the street daily. The teen grew excited about running and decided to try out for the school track team. He went on to set several track records for his high school and, later, for his university.

I have also noticed that toe walkers sometimes have tight, inflexible hips, which improves with exercises, stretching, and inhibition of the Spinal Galant and Symmetrical Tonic Neck reflexes. Every toe-walking child I have met has also shown very tight hamstrings and calf muscles. As these reflexes withdraw, back leg stretches are often necessary.

Spinal Galant Reflex

> The Spinal Galant Reflex appears to be involved during the birth process as it allows small rotational movements of the baby's pelvis on either side as it works its way down the birth canal…. It has also been suggested that this reflex may conduct sound **in utero** as it vibrates up through the body.[3]

This reflex emerges in the womb and should withdraw by three to nine months after birth. In my experience, children seem to either have a fully retained Spinal Galant Reflex or none at all. Few seem to partly retain it. Children with this reflex are often wiggly, wiggly, wiggly! Tags, waistbands, backs of chairs — anything that touches the lumbar area near the spine — tickle or aggravate and cause the hips to reflexively jerk. Many of these children continue to wet the bed beyond the normal age. These children sometimes pull tags off their clothes, or play with waistband clothing tags. When my daughter was seven, she would suck her thumb and twirl the waist tag at the back of her pants or skirt.

The waistline area is sensitive, so some children prefer clothes that are loose-fitting at the waist, such as sweats or elasticized waistbands. Others prefer jeans that are baggy in the waist. Either way, clothing near the waist is often a bother.

Children with this reflex may do schoolwork with better focus and attention if they can sit or lie on their tummies on the floor so they are less susceptible to irritations along the lumbar region.

With inhibition of the Spinal Galant Reflex, some children stop bedwetting literally overnight; with others, it is a long, continuing problem. Inhibition of this reflex does not guarantee children will stop bedwetting, but many do.

In my experience, children frequently show inhibition of the Rooting, Palmar, Plantar, and Spinal Galant reflexes at about the same time that the Moro and Tonic Labyrinthine reflexes inhibit. Every child seems to progress through NDD therapy in his or her own manner, however, as no two children are the same.

Chapter 6

Asymmetrical Tonic Neck Reflex

This reflex can be observed in a newborn by turning her head to one side. The arm and leg on the same side extend and the arm and leg on the opposite side bend. Where the head goes, the arm and eyes go.[4]

The Asymmetrical Tonic Neck Reflex (ATNR) begins in the womb and typically withdraws at about six months of age. Infants often sleep in the position of this reflex. Inhibition of this and other primitive reflexes stimulate development of eye movements. A newborn gradually becomes able to focus and make eye contact, convergence develops, and soon the child is able to track objects with his or her eyes. As this reflex withdraws, later development is initiated such as creeping and crawling, crossing of midline (e.g., crossing arms or ankles, or when the eyes read left to right), laterality (dominant side), the ability to multi-task (think and do at the same time), and finally academic achievement.

During a child's NDD therapy program, the ATNR is a reflex parents frequently ask about. Experience suggests this is because emotionally and behaviorally the child is more settled (the Moro and TLR show substantial withdrawal) and parental concerns for their children likewise transition from emotional or behavioral stability to academics. Retention of this reflex nearly always affects academics. I have not yet seen a child who was diagnosed with dyslexia or dysgraphia and did not have this reflex. When parents ask me about these diagnoses, I share that in each case I have encountered, retention of the ATNR and other primitive reflexes (and possibly auditory processing struggles) combine to produce the symptoms of dyslexia. Later, as the reflexes withdraw, and auditory processing improves, the original symptoms either decrease significantly or disappear altogether. Retention of the ATNR may heavily impact academic performance.

Body Positions

I have seen many individuals whose hands or arms involuntarily show mirrored (imitation) movements when the ATNR shows a residual presence. I remember when my granddaughter, about 18 months of age, had learned what "shake" means. She loved grabbing noisy objects, and when I said, "Shake," she would shake them up and down with delight. Interestingly, when she shook an object in one hand, the other hand mirrored the movement as if she held an object in each hand and shook them simultaneously. This is normal in a child of that age. As my granddaughter neared the age of two, she showed less and less mirroring of the hands and arms. By age two-and-a-half, she no longer involuntarily mirrored hands or arms.

Hand mirroring, however, is sometimes observed in older children. I met a teenager who could easily teach himself to play interesting and varied instruments. Each time he came for an office visit, he performed on instruments such as a Vietnamese jaw harp and an asalato. He plays piano but described his frustration with trying to play. He said he could play each hand individually but was unable to play both hands simultaneously. When both hands were on the keys, they naturally wanted to mirror movements. As he described this to me, I was convinced it was related to his retention of the ATNR. As the ATNR started to withdraw, he commented that he had noticed an increased ability to play instruments with each hand moving independently. After just a few months of starting NDD therapy, he came to my office one day with an ocarina (an instrument that I thought looked like a plastic sweet potato with strategically placed holes) and played a Celtic song. He was excited to show me that his fingers played simultaneously, independently, and rapidly. Fingers on one hand no longer mirrored finger movements of the opposite hand.

Children may demonstrate awkward body positions during drawing, writing, or other hand-eye coordination projects. Some children lift the shoulder of the dominant hand while using that hand, and the opposite shoulder may drop or hunch. It is common to see awkward torso, shoulder, arm, and/or hand positions until the reflex withdraws.

Many individuals with a retained ATNR are uncomfortable with sitting cross-legged. Positions on the floor are often anything but crossing the lower legs with bent knees. For a time, these children are usually not comfortable sitting on chairs either. Their bodies are most comfortable in positions that

> Their bodies are most comfortable in positions that others may think are awkward or distracting.

others may think are awkward or distracting. I have temporarily seated some of these children on stools so their feet can dangle, or given them a rug in order to sit in a specified space however they chose. When allowed to sit in these positions, their pencil-to-paper work and ability to focus improved. As the reflex withdraws, body positions in the upper and lower torso begin to look more natural and comfortable.

Head and Eye Movements

Signs of the continued presence of the ATNR include body movements that occur in response to side-to-side head movements. When the head turns, the body, shoulders, and/or arms reflexively turn as one with the head. Balance may be compromised from head turns to either side. Retention of this reflex particularly affects eye tracking and hand-eye tracking, both of which are necessary for good reading and writing. A child who skips words, lines, parts of words, or suffixes while reading usually shows poor eye tracking. Some children show difficulty with reading comprehension for a time because their eyes are struggling to follow a line of print and therefore the ability to think and process the text at the same time becomes overwhelming.

> ...when a child shows impaired eye tracking and hand-eye tracking, my goal is not to provide exercises for improved eye movements, but to stimulate the Asymmetrical Tonic Neck Reflex into withdrawal.

These are not visual problems per se, but areas that improve as the reflex withdraws. So when a child shows impaired eye tracking and hand-eye tracking, my goal is not to provide exercises for improved eye movements, but to stimulate the Asymmetrical Tonic Neck Reflex into withdrawal. In my experience, as the reflex inhibits, eye movements have consistently improved.

Academics

Children with a continued presence of the Asymmetrical Tonic Neck Reflex typically struggle in many areas academically. The ability to multi-task is compromised. Until the body is able to multi-task, the brain seems to struggle with it as well. Eye movements such as tracking and hand-eye tracking are difficult, especially when the child tries to converse while tracking. I have seen this directly correlate to an inability to think and write at the same time. The eyes move with the head, arm, or torso and cannot track unless all conscious effort is put into it. Conversation or thinking processes either cease or the tracking ceases when verbalization starts.

These children often write poorly or dislike writing. Sentences may be poorly constructed and lack appropriate grammar, syntax, punctuation, and/or spelling. Expressing ideas verbally and/or on paper is difficult. I share with parents that it is as if, when asked to write a sentence, a child subconsciously says, "Pick one — creativity, grammar, syntax, punctuation, or spelling. You will only get one, so pick which one you want."

For these children, depending on the level of severity, I either suggest writing be put on hold for a time and, as much as possible, assignments be done verbally, or that the child should dictate and an adult scribe. The beginning stages of writing occur when creativity is stimulated. Allowing a child to dictate a story or event provides the opportunity for stimulation of creativity. The child is able to focus on his thoughts and ideas without having to slow down to write. For the time being, this eliminates the sense of being overwhelmed by, for example, attempting to spell correctly while trying to remember the numerous components of good sentence structure, such as grammar and punctuation. I typically find that children use higher vocabulary when dictating at this stage because they do not have to be concerned about spelling.

When the ATNR is less severe, I may suggest that the child be asked to write a sentence and the assisting adult say, "Now, go back and look for anything you want to change regarding capitals and periods." When that is done, say, "Now, go back and check your spelling, slowly and carefully one word at a time." This continues with each area of writing so that the child handles only one task at a time.

Some children initially show this reflex in their handwriting. For example, they may start writing at the middle of the paper instead of at the left margin. One first-grade boy I met started writing at the left margin, stopped as he neared the middle of the paper, and then began again about four inches to the right of the previous word. His finished paper showed writing on the left side of the paper and also on the right side, but nothing down the middle. Each eye tracked to midline, or away from midline, but not across midline. As the Asymmetrical Tonic Neck Reflex withdrew, his writing reflected the change. Several months later I showed him his initial paper and he said it could not have been his — he would never write with a gap down the middle of his paper!

I have seen right-handed individuals who, when standing at a chalkboard or white board, begin writing at the midline point of their own body and continue to their right instead of crossing midline with the right hand to start writing on the left side of the board. The information from the viewer's perspective was written from the middle of the board to the right and the left side remained vacant. Children with this reflex often do not start their writing at the left margin of their paper.

Reading in an older child usually shows compensation techniques that later hold the child back once this reflex has withdrawn. They enter a phase in which compensation techniques need to be eliminated so that good reading skills can become natural. I have not yet seen that visual, whole-word, or context reading benefit these children. Picture-word reading does not help them in the long run. These children usually advance in reading quite well when they break up old habits, slow down, and start sounding words out, even if it means going back to rudimentary reading for a while. Reading has to be learned sound-by-sound; every letter should be sounded out and words that are skipped or misread should be corrected. Slow, accurate reading precedes fluid reading, and fluid reading precedes comprehension. I have seen it come together, in time, for countless children.

A child with this reflex may initially struggle with multiple directions given at the same time, such as, "Clear the table, rinse out the bowls, and put them in the dishwasher." Often, this also indicates an auditory processing problem, but in some cases, slowing down and giving one instruction at a time lessens the level of frustration for parents, teachers, and children. On occasion, this improves as the ATNR withdraws, but in most cases it does not improve until after completion of the listening therapy.

Physical Activities

Sports frequently improve as this reflex withdraws. Children naturally become more comfortable with using a dominant hand or foot and crossing midline looks more comfortable and fluid. At this point, many children better understand symmetry within their own bodies and it shows in coordination. I remember a father who called one day to tell me he was thrilled to be watching his 11-year-old daughter roller skate (at that very moment) with a natural stride for the first time in her life. Another dad wiped tears from his eyes one day as he described how his 12-year-old son comfortably and fluidly crossed midline with his hockey stick and made his first goal. My daughter crossed her legs instinctively while sitting in a chair for the first time at age 21.

Withdrawal of this reflex is crucial in order to achieve improved coordination and academics. It must be remembered that in normal development this reflex withdraws prior to a child's development of side dominance, crossing of midline, and ability to multi-task — all related to physical coordination and academic pursuits. Many parents have demonstrated tremendous trust when I encouraged them to wait to attempt reading, writing, spelling, or math; when their children were ready and the process began, they realized the wait had not been in vain. I frequently hear parents describe changes they observe in their children regarding handwriting and paragraph writing. Letter and word spacing improve, neatness and letter formation is refined, and writing becomes more fluid. Some children start journaling on their own initiative. Others start writing stories and creating their own story books.

As this reflex withdraws, many children begin to show abilities in areas that none of us — parents, teachers, siblings, extended family, and even the children themselves — would ever have guessed were inside waiting to bloom. Some become gifted students, talented writers, excellent debaters, winners of essay contests, artists, and spectacular athletes. Others come out of special education programs, and that is a reward in itself. Others become average students. Some continue to have difficulties but significantly less severe. In any case, previously hidden talents and abilities beautifully emerge as the ATNR withdraws.

Chapter 7

Symmetrical Tonic Neck Reflex

The Symmetric Tonic Neck Reflex (STNR) appears between six and nine months of age, remains for two or three months and then withdraws. This reflex causes an infant to position himself on his hands and knees in preparation for creeping and eventually walking. The head goes back, the upper half of the body straightens and the lower half bends. When the head goes down, the upper half of the body goes with it and the legs begin to extend.[5]

Toddlers often sit on their haunches and then may lift their rear ends and rock back and forth before they begin to creep on their hands and knees. As they rapidly and eagerly move about on all fours, the hands are loose and flat, the feet are relaxed and on the floor, the back is straight, and the arms and legs move in a synchronized cross pattern. This stimulates independent use of the upper and lower halves of the body. As children work through the process of this reflex, the eyes should develop the ability to cross midline, look up at what is ahead, and the eyes and hands begin to coordinate. This process is a precursor to necessary abilities for reading, writing, copying, balance, and space and depth perception.

All of the primitive reflexes previously discussed

emerge in the womb and then, in normal development, withdraw before children are one year of age — before they sit in chairs with their feet on the floor, before walking, and often before beginning to creep on all fours (some may inhibit during the creeping stage). The STNR bridges from the primitive into the postural reflexes. It should withdraw prior to or at about the time a child begins to walk. It impacts a child's posture, eye movements, coordination, and balance.

Posture

Postures of children with this reflex are varied and typically frustrating for parents and teachers. Children with a strong presence of the STNR are typically not comfortable in chairs and become fidgety. Various expressions of poor posture include sitting on their feet,

> Children with a strong presence of the STNR are typically not comfortable in chairs and become fidgety.

sitting with their legs in a W position, fidgetiness in chairs, not sitting still at the dinner table, or a preference for standing at the dinner table or at their desks at school. When seated, they typically prefer to sit with their calves near their thighs so that the inside angle behind each knee is closed or nearly closed. Limited hip rotation, tight hamstrings, and tight calves often accompany the continued presence of this reflex. As the STNR begins to withdraw, many children also need to do leg stretches for the calves and hamstrings.

These children may have rounded torsos and seem unable to pull their shoulders back. They round their backs over the dinner table, over their desk at school, or pull their knees into their chests and round their torsos to or over their knees. Others like to lie on their tummies with bent elbows. While on their tummies, their knees often bend and feet float in the air, or the knees bend, feet go to the floor, and their bottoms go into the air. Parents who desire healthier attitudes and attention to school work often find that children with a strong STNR perform better when allowed to get comfortable on the floor before starting their work. As the reflex withdraws, children typically initiate a desire to move from the floor to a chair.

I repeatedly say throughout a child's therapy program, however, that we will get to these postural concerns later on in the program because up until this point we are helping the child to retrace the steps that would have occurred in normal development in the natural order. The STNR bridges a child from the floor to seated, standing, and walking postures; all of the other reflexes we have discussed emerge and withdraw prior to this in normal development, so they must be addressed first. As a result, this reflex typically inhibits near the final months of a child's NDD therapy.

Eye Movements

Academics are often affected because of posture problems, as well as from possible eye movement difficulties that usually accompany this reflex. Copying is commonly difficult – the eyes are unable to make smooth pursuit from paper on a desk or table to a textbook and back or to a board on the wall and back. Parents may wonder why the work is such a problem for a smart child and may complain, "But all you had to do was copy it. Why is that so difficult?" It is! If the eyes do not make smooth pursuit back and forth, children might make numerous mistakes while copying; they may skip words or lines, show inadequate spacing of letters or words, omit letters or words, or show tremendous fatigue or frustration from the task in general. They may procrastinate and dilly-dally instead of getting the work done.

I remember an eight-year-old who was near completion of NDD therapy. Her posture was good, academics were good, emotions were stable, but I tested and found that the Symmetrical Tonic Neck Reflex was more evident than I would have liked. I asked her to copy a paragraph from a grade-level book. Her numerous copying mistakes told me she needed to work through this reflex a bit longer. I suggested her mother check her daughter's copying work periodically and watch for natural, gradual improvement. Within a short time, the reflex fully withdrew and her copying work, handwriting, and attention to detail while writing all improved.

Vertical tracking is another eye movement related to the STNR. Until this reflex withdraws, some children struggle with aligning numbers in math. The longer the chain of numbers to line up for addition, the more difficult it becomes for the child to do the math. The problem is not necessarily being able to add several numbers but trying to line up the numbers on paper. Parents and teachers may provide graph paper or turn lined paper sideways so the lines run vertically and columns become available. Once this reflex shows substantial withdrawal, I hear about better vertical alignment without special accommodations.

Coordination and Balance

Sports activities generally improve dramatically as this reflex withdraws. Parents repeatedly share stories about how much more fluidly their children move while running, swimming, skating, or skiing. Improved coordination overall allows many to excel in their favorite sports. I remember working with a girl who struggled with incoordination and balance, yet several years later became a competitive ballet dancer. Another teen, clumsy and uncoordinated, joined her swim team at school and became one of the best on the team. Relatives of one teen boy were astounded at the young man's sudden improvement in skiing. Another teen improved significantly in soccer and was chosen to try out for the Olympic soccer team. Not every child who shows inhibition of this and other reflexes becomes a star athlete. Many do, and others show more fluid movements in daily activities. My daughter is not an athlete, but she was ecstatic the first time she was able to do jumping jacks, and so was I.

Inhibition of the primitive reflexes and stimulation of the brain stem brings out a child's potential, whatever that child's potential might be. As my daughter completed NDD therapy, I did not think, Hmm, there's still something else going on. No longer did I wonder what might still be lurking underneath as I had with previous interventions. My daughter is whole, her potential shows, and I am delighted. I see this in other children as well. I think parents know and sense with satisfaction when their child begins to reveal his or her potential.

PART 3: INTERACTIONS

Chapter 8

One Thing Leads to Another:
Emergence of the Postural Reflexes

In normal development, the postural reflexes begin to emerge in the first few months after birth and as the primitive reflexes withdraw. They should be fully mature by the time children are three years old. These are called postural reflexes because they are related to postural positions required for gross motor movements as well as muscle tone, voluntary body positions, and movements for sitting, standing, walking, running — activities that children are expected to begin once they are mobile enough to sit, then stand and walk, and play.

Older children who show the continued presence of primitive reflexes usually also show delay in development of the postural reflexes. I find this to be true regardless of how much intervention a child has experienced. I believe this is why some of these children have awkward stances, limited hip rotation, and tight muscles particularly in the legs.

As older children show inhibition of the primitive reflexes through NDD therapy, they generally start showing signs of emerging postural reflexes. I watch for these to begin developing naturally, indicating maturation within the central nervous system. Withdrawal of the primitive reflexes should stimulate maturity just as it does in normal development. In my experience, the postural reflexes nearly always, at a minimum, begin to develop during an individual's NDD therapy program. The amount of stimulation needed to bring about full maturity varies between children.

Head Righting Reflexes

Head righting reflexes have to do with natural sensing of head position when the torso or body is not aligned. For example, when riding a bicycle, the rider leans into turns and makes continual body adjustments for balance while riding. When seated in a boat out on the water, body adjustments are made as the boat sways or lifts on the waves. Anytime a body is stationary while on a moving apparatus, instinctive adjustments should occur. The head should naturally align itself so that if the body moves — or gets pushed — in any direction, the head reflexively maintains a straight and centered position in order to maintain balance. If it does not, the individual may struggle to maintain balance, become dizzy, or fall. In my experience, motion sickness is often related to this. If a child becomes dizzy or nauseous while riding in a car — from quick stops or curvy mountain roads — I find that, in nearly every case, the child does not have properly developed head righting reflexes.

I hear children tell me they get headaches in their classrooms and the headaches go away once school is out for the day. If I hear this complaint after the primitive reflexes are nearly fully withdrawn, I typically find the head righting reflexes have not fully emerged. These children consistently roll their eyes up to look at me, at the teacher, or at the board while copying. They do not lift their heads to look straight ahead.

Head righting reflexes are critical for stability and vision, but also require vestibular stability. Some children are able to instinctively right their heads when their eyes are open, but as soon as they close their eyes, they lose sense of their bodies or heads in space. Their heads no longer reflexively respond.

As the head righting reflexes mature, confidence in body movements is usually observed, as well as improvements in academics and sports activities. As children show development of these reflexes, they generally show increased confidence in body movements.

Amphibian Reflex

The Amphibian Reflex stimulates integration of each side of the body. When each hip is elevated from a supine position, the corresponding knee should reflexively bend. I have met countless children well beyond the age in which this should be a natural movement continue to struggle with natural hip, leg, and knee responses. The legs are often stiff and awkward in movements and do not seem to know how to work with arm movements — either similar or opposing movements. As a result, a soldier crawl across the floor looks uncoordinated and incongruous. Creeping on hands and knees is often unsynchronized as well. When I meet a child who shows this reflex to be significantly underdeveloped, I nearly always find the child also shows the continued presence of the Tonic Labyrinthine Reflex and the Asymmetrical Tonic Neck Reflex. As the two primitive reflexes withdraw, the Amphibian Reflex usually begins to emerge.

Segmental Rolling Reflex

The Segmental Rolling Reflex is a postural reflex that allows coordinated rolling from the tummy to the back and vice versa. Many children demonstrate uncoordinated, stiff, log roll movements. The upper and lower halves of the body do not coordinate and it shows in sports and day-to-day activities. I have worked with teens who love particular sports but their coaches complain about this very problem. As the teens worked through the postural reflexes, their arms and legs, sides, and upper and lower halves became more fluid, coordinated, and synchronized.

I have found that, for some children, the primitive reflexes become nearly fully withdrawn yet the postural reflexes do not fully develop during their NDD therapy program. This has, in some cases, proved to be a good time for a break from therapy. Many of these children and teens continue development. Over time, and without any further intervention, the postural reflexes mature naturally. These children are often involved in Martial Arts. I have known a few who showed emergence of the postural reflexes through swimming. Other children seem to plateau — They do not regress, nor do they show continued development of the postural reflexes. After several months of waiting to see what a child's body does, parents and I are able to ascertain whether or not a child needs assistance in order to stimulate further development of the postural reflexes.

Several years ago, I visited Scotland and learned about Sheila Dobie's Bilateral Integration program.* It is by far the best therapy program I have seen that stimulates the postural reflexes and overall coordination. As children have become proficient in carrying out these exercises, they have shown tremendous improvement in emergence of the postural reflexes, coordination, and joint mobility. Many become significantly better athletes in whatever sport they choose.

---

*Sheila Dobie Associate (Training) Ltd., Bo'ness, Scotland

Chapter 9

The Day Car Washes Became "No Big Deal": The Vestibular System and How it Interacts with NDD

An adequately functioning vestibular system allows efficient processing of sensory impulses. As the primitive reflexes withdraw, the vestibular system is stimulated. I have observed that the reverse may also occur — when the vestibular system is stimulated at early stages of normal development, the primitive reflexes may be stimulated toward maturity.

> The vestibular system is the unifying system. It forms the basic relationship of a person to gravity and the physical world. All other types of sensation are processed in reference to this basic vestibular information. The activity in the vestibular system provides a "framework" for the other aspects of our experience. Vestibular input seems to "prime" the entire nervous system to function effectively. When the vestibular system does not function in a consistent and accurate way, the interpretation of other sensations will be inconsistent and inaccurate, and the nervous system will have trouble "getting started."[6]

The vestibular system begins to develop early within an unborn child, and proper development is crucially related to development of other parts of the central nervous system. Use of medications during the first few weeks of pregnancy can damage the vestibular system.[7]

Development of the vestibular system begins in the inner ear and then proceeds at a faster rate than the auditory system. While its nucleus is in the brain stem, the three organs of the vestibular apparatus are the semicircular canals inside the ear. Messages are sent from neurons inside the canals to the midbrain, brain stem, and spinal cord, allowing for head movements forward and backward, side to side, and tilting (ear toward the shoulder). At ten weeks after conception, a fetus should be able to respond to movement stimulation. By 12 weeks the eyes should move reflexively when the head turns. A baby in the womb should orient himself to the pull of gravity and turn so that his head is down a few weeks prior to birth. "Indeed, babies born with defects in their vestibular system have a much greater chance of being in a breech position, presumably because they can't adequately discern the difference between up and down."[8]

Because the vestibular system provides this foundational framework, it directly affects an individual's sense of proprioception, space perception, visual and auditory processing, and balance. Sleep and wake cycles, REM dream sleep, and digestion are also interrelated with the vestibular system. It affects muscle tone, fear (or lack of fear) of heights, and energy levels. It enables a child to determine her own body position in space. It impacts sensory experiences, balance required for standing, walking, running and more mature physical activities, orientation and the ability to turn things in space, regulation of attention span, and reading an analog clock. The vestibular system interconnects with the ability to sequence and grasp inverse operations in math such as addition versus subtraction or multiplication versus division. A dysfunctional vestibular system may negatively affect one or more of these innate body functions.

Proprioception

Proprioception is the ability to recognize one's body and body parts in space, whether at rest or during movement. Muscle and joint sensations help an individual determine body movements, which leads to appropriate use of the extremities for handling utensils, running, climbing, play, as well as sitting at a desk and holding one's head up. A child with poor vestibular proprioception is often clumsy, perhaps always moving about in order to "find himself." I see children daily who are unable to accurately touch their nose, or the opposite hand, or a knee without looking directly at what they are doing. Many are also unable to accurately recognize touch unless they can see where they have been touched. Low muscle tone may also be a factor. A child may have poor posture and low energy so that holding a pencil or holding his head up is too much work. Most children I work with show improved proprioception during NDD therapy.

My own daughter changed dramatically. Stimulation at the brain stem level initiated proprioceptive development, and we observed changes in her body awareness. As a child she did not back up to sit on chairs; she faced a chair and usually placed one bent knee on the chair and then turned and sat on her foot. As long as she faced the chair and could see it, she planted herself onto the chair. She easily fell off chairs, too. I watched my 15-

month-old granddaughter play with proprioception at her young age. She often walked backward and as she became aware of a step, small stool, or pillow behind her, she plopped down. She frequently sat on the floor and slowly lowered her spine; when her spine was flat on the floor, she then lowered her head to the floor. The entire process was slow and controlled. She knew where her body parts were without having to see them and planned her movements accordingly. She often handed me a string necklace and then tipped her head forward so that I would put the necklace over her head and around her neck. While she knew where her body parts were at 15 months of age, my daughter's proprioception did not develop appropriately until she was between the ages of 18-21.

Space Perception

Space perception is directly related to vestibular function. The ability to rotate objects in space, understand the difference between push and pull, and have a sense of direction are all affected by the vestibular system. Seemingly simple tasks such as playing catch, stacking blocks, pasting objects onto paper, shaping letters and/or numbers in the right direction, and knowing the perimeters of one's backyard or a designated area at a park can be extremely difficult or impossible for those with spatial difficulties.

My daughter could not walk to the end of the block in our neighborhood and know how to find her way back home. She could not separate from me in the toy department of a store for fear of not finding me again. She was fearful of being in the car when we went through a car wash because in her mind the roller brushes came through the windshield straight at her. Letters and numbers were consistently written backward, even when she was a teenager.

Naturally, we had assumed that our daughter would never drive a car. Although we pushed her to try it a few times, she was unable to judge distances, froze when another moving car appeared, and did not know how to judge the turning of the steering wheel. She was just as lost in the driver's seat as she was inside her own body.

As we observed spatial changes over time from stimulation at the brain stem level, we were excited at how fast and varied the changes were. She began to voluntarily separate from me in stores to do her own shopping and suggest a place where we could later meet up again. She volunteered to go into grocery stores on her own to buy items on my list (and she knew where to find the items). Car washes became "no big deal." She often walked to the nearby park and rode her bike around the neighborhood by herself. Letters and numbers were no longer reversed in her writing. Actions that seem "simple" excited me because they demonstrated profound changes. One day I laughed with delight when I watched her exhibit yet another perfect example of spatial awareness. I was parked in the driveway waiting for her to join me in the car. She came out of the garage holding the garage-door remote. As she came out of the garage, she lifted her arm so that the remote was above and behind her, and she clicked the button so that the garage door closed. Not only did she not turn around to make sure she was no longer inside the garage, she did not have to face the garage in order to close the door with the remote. This would not have happened prior to NDD therapy. She now has her driver's license. I am eternally grateful for the miraculous changes we have seen in our own daughter, not just for our benefit, but for hers. She has a future. A future we were told she would never experience.

Many daily activities require space perception, including processing of information that refers to spatial concepts. My daughter has taken up cross-stitching and one day asked me to help her with part of the project. I casually said, "On this part, you would go up ten and over six." She immediately responded, "I get it. This is one thing I would not have been able to do in the past. I wouldn't have known what you meant by 'up' and 'over.'"

Math can be impacted by poor space perception. Many children struggle with inverse operations such as addition versus subtraction or multiplication versus division. Or, some subtract a smaller digit from the larger digit in multi-digit problems regardless of which is the larger whole number. Many older children continue to struggle with understanding place value (e.g., hundreds, tens, and ones). Some children struggle with understanding the purpose of the equals sign. In earlier math, they often define the equals sign as meaning, "And the answer is...." This misperception becomes especially problematic when they begin algebra. They do not yet see that the goal is to maintain balance on both sides, of an equation, and therefore, "What is done to one side must also be done to the other side." Rather, they are often thinking in frustration, "If I need the answer to this algebra problem, why would I keep adding or subtracting numbers to both sides?"

> Math can be impacted by poor space perception.

Reading and writing may also be affected by poor space perception. I have worked with children who struggled with knowing where to start reading the text after turning the page in a book, not realizing that text consistently begins on the left side. They may upturn letters such as "m" and "w" or reverse letters such as "b" and "d" or "p" and "q." When writing, they may pull out a piece of lined notebook paper and write on the back side instead of the front. My daughter never could grasp which side of the paper was the front, and all her written work up through high school was done on the back side of her notebook paper. I am thrilled that this simple part of writing on paper is now consistently correct and taken for granted.

The Visual System

The visual system also interconnects with the vestibular system and sends information to the brain stem for processing. Development of eye movements and later postural abilities are affected by maturity of the vestibular system. Possible delay in development of the vestibular system in a newborn or infant often shows in a lack of visual alertness. I often see a continued lack of visual alertness in older children, which, in my experience, has consistently proved to be one of several dysfunctions that pointed to neuro-developmental delay.

Balance may be affected by eye movements. I have worked with many children who initially swayed whenever one eye was covered while the other eye tracked an object. As the vestibular system showed maturity, the sway disappeared. Many children are unable to track an object with their eyes alone. In other words, where the head goes, the eyes go; or where the eyes go, the head goes — a cohesive movement. In my experience, eye movements become independent of head movements as the primitive reflexes withdraw and the vestibular system matures.

The Auditory System

The auditory and vestibular systems intersect. Signals travel to and from the vestibular system in the inner ear through the nucleus of the vestibular system in the brain stem. Language comprehension, speech irregularities, articulation, clear discrimination of sounds, and processing of information depend upon adequate functioning of the vestibular and auditory systems. Many children I work with show auditory processing difficulties. Most show slight improvement in auditory processing from vestibular stimulation and NDD therapy, and sound/listening therapy (described in greater detail in the following chapter) is often required. I remember a teenager whose parents were frustrated by his lack of communication. They were accustomed to painfully slow, one-word answers. On his last day of the listening therapy, I asked him to verbally summarize for his parents the first few chapters of a book he had read to me during the previous several days. His parents were astounded at how well he shared what he had read, and his mother, with tears in her eyes, said she had never heard that much communication from her son at one time.

I remember working with a three-year-old girl who was referred to me from Child Find.* The girl was principally nonverbal, and the one or two words she occasionally said were unclear. For example, instead of saying "water," she, much like a young toddler, said, "wa." I showed her parents one vestibular exercise to do with her daily for the next few months, and then she started the listening therapy. Before she completed the 60-hour program, she had begun to clearly enunciate and articulate thoughts and desires. Her family and extended family were astounded. Several months later, her mother jokingly shared that they once worried about her not talking, and now they did not know how to get her to stop talking.

Balance

Balance is consistently dysfunctional in children with neuro-developmental delay. Although many parents tell me prior to our first meeting that their children are quite athletic and have excellent balance, I find that aspects of balance are actually impaired. Some children show difficulties related to static balance, dynamic balance, midline balance, or a combination of the three.

---

*Child-Find is a service provided by school districts of Boards of Cooperative Educational Services (BOCES). The district or board of professionals are trained to evaluate children in a variety of areas, including cognitive functioning, physical functioning, hearing and vision, speech and language and social and emotional development.

Static balance is the ability to maintain balance when the body is not moving. Children who may easily be able to ride a bicycle or skateboard may still struggle with static balance. Many children who seem hyper and busy with their bodies also show poor static balance. They sway and fidget and may nearly fall over when asked to stand still with their feet together and arms by their sides. When standing on one foot, they may hop about or flail their arms in an effort to maintain balance. In my experience, these children tend to show increased difficulty with maintaining balance when they close their eyes; they often lose their balance when standing still with their eyes closed.

Dynamic balance is balance during movement. Dynamic balance difficulties may show in children who are slow at learning to ride a bicycle, or struggle when they walk backward, on their toes, or across a beam. Maintaining balance during movement is difficult, and most likely, increasingly difficult when attempting to carry out the movement backward, without visual cues.

Midline balance difficulties are usually part of static or dynamic balance difficulties. Children may show good static balance overall, but the closer their feet come to midline, the more difficult balance becomes. I have observed that some have found ways to compensate, such as by widening their stance or turning the toes (or the heels) outward away from midline. I have watched as some children maintain static balance until one or both arms cross midline, then lose or nearly lose their balance.

So, while balance may be stable in one area, it is often poor in another area. Balance may look good until one's eyes close or until the head turns. I have seen many children lose their balance when their heads are in any position other than facing straight ahead, in line with their spine. Many children who show the continued presence of several of the primitive reflexes also struggle with balance.

The Digestive System

The digestive system also interacts with the vestibular system. Many children I work with suffer from motion sickness, either from sudden starts and stops, or curvy roads, or both. Older children often tell me they cannot read while in the car, or they have to be able to watch the road ahead in order to avoid getting sick. Because the vagus nerve travels from the brain stem to major organs of the body, vestibular imbalances (also rooted in the brain stem) may affect the stomach and digestion.

Dizziness or a lack of dizziness can create nausea — a vestibular and vagus nerve-related problem. I worked with a 21-year-old whose only difficulty was motion sickness. She hated riding in cars and took Dramamine when she flew. If she did not take Dramamine and sleep on airplanes, she vomited in her seat. After a few short months of one vestibular exercise, her motion sickness drastically reduced and she could fly on planes without putting herself to sleep. She still does not read while riding in a car, but she called me one day to tell me she rode on several roller coaster rides at an amusement park, and for the first time ever, it was fun and she did not get sick. As children continue with their NDD therapy I listen for accounts of dizziness from those who previously never got dizzy; or a lack of dizziness from those who struggled with being overly dizzy. Many parents excitedly share that they notice their children no longer suffer with motion sickness and family car journeys have become more doable.

Some children experience short periods of nausea from a specific NDD exercise. I have seen this work itself out so that the nausea dissipates. This seems to coincide with Moro Reflex withdrawal and vestibular system stabilization.

Vestibular Stimulation

Generally, children's programs regarding vestibular therapy include balance and eye movements. Stimulation often includes spinning, rocking, rolling, jumping up and down, running, dancing, riding a bicycle, walking a balance beam, etc. Some activities combine eye movements such as tracking an object while jumping or moving in some way. These are all activities of an older child. Many children, however, show dysfunction of the vestibular system from an earlier age. *Anna's House* begins with stimulation at these earlier stages of development.

Every single child I have worked with has shown some sort of vestibular dysfunction. One must keep in mind the specific areas within the vestibular system that show dysfunction within a given individual because they collectively interrelate. Dysfunction in these areas manifests in various combinations and at varying intensities: sensory, tactile, auditory, visual, balance, body awareness, body image, spatial awareness, and proprioception. Stimulation should be specific and with careful movement when dysfunction begins at the brain stem level.

Vestibular stimulation at early stages of development requires careful, deliberate movement. Babies move about slowly in a confined space prior to birth. Shortly after birth, they are handled gently when moved, rocked, or soothed. As babies mature, faster and more aggressive movements begin such as bouncing or swinging. In my experience, precise movements that stimulate early stages of development have activated maturity of the vestibular system in older children. As children participate in their own specific exercise, many demonstrate pre-birth, embryonic responses. Reactions, during or immediately following the vestibular exercise, are as varied as the number of children. Overall, many show fetal positions, cocooning-type positions, rooting, irregular breathing much like a newborn, an infant startle, the Spinal Galant Reflex, or the Tonic Labyrinthine Reflex. In time, I have seen these children mature rapidly in balance, body awareness, motor movements, behavior, and academics — all from careful, deliberate vestibular stimulation.

The amount of stimulation required also varies from person to person. I have seen some children overstimulated by a given exercise so that they become incredibly excited and over active or the opposite — sullen and morose for a short time. While some need the stimulation to slowly increase over time, others respond at a different pace. Just as exercises that stimulate withdrawal of the primitive reflexes vary per child, exercises for particular vestibular stimulation also vary according to an individual's needs.

A Medley of Growth

In my experience, changes in the vestibular system

vary per person for those experiencing NDD therapy. Some show remarkable vestibular changes immediately. Others show a slow, steady pace. Others fluctuate up and down and then stabilize toward the end. I remember a family in which I worked with three of the four siblings. All three children showed periodic vestibular disruption — balance seemed to have regressed, they walked into doors, and they misjudged their bodies in space. In each child, it lasted for a short period, only to repeat the cycle again later. As I followed and retested, I found that every time each of the children experienced a significant change (such as one or two of the primitive reflexes showed substantial steps toward withdrawal), their vestibular system showed disruption for a short period. As each child neared completion of NDD therapy, their vestibular system showed maturity and stability.

Children may show social or behavioral improvements from vestibular stimulation at the brain stem level, but academics may continue to lag for a time. Some children continue to reverse letters or numbers, or processing of information is slow to develop. For others, academics is not a problem, but body awareness and social behaviors lag. Parents need to realize that changes cannot be expected to come all at once or all at the same time. I habitually encourage parents to reevaluate the normal pattern of development and observe their children closely. Watch for the next developmental stage to emerge.

A mother whose daughter was suddenly able to count was discouraged because her daughter could not count in rhythm or touch-count. I asked the girl to count my fingers as I held them out in front of her. The touches did not match her counting, and she counted nine fingers even though she touched all ten. I perceived this as vestibular dysfunction and suggested that the mother touch objects while the daughter counted instead of having the daughter touch the objects while counting. I then held the girl's hands so that her fingers were stiffly splayed. As I touched each of her fingers one at a time, she counted accurately. I then touch-counted flowers on her shirt, and she felt the touches. When her vestibular system showed more maturity, I then observed she could touch-count easily and accurately.

> ...changes in vestibular function at the brain stem level have correlated with children's abilities to use verb tenses correctly.

During the listening therapy, vestibular changes are often noted. The children engage in quiet activities while undergoing the therapy, and many like to play board games. Often, they are at first unable to count and move their markers along the matching number of spaces. They count aloud but move their markers randomly. It is not unusual to see these children begin to count in synchrony with movements of their markers before they finish the listening therapy. Many children also begin to assemble jigsaw puzzles. They suddenly grasp the difference between border and inside pieces and notice that shape is as critical to finding the right piece as color. I have seen children who initially were unable to do a puzzle easily and quickly assemble a 100-piece puzzle.

Interestingly, changes in vestibular function at the brain stem level have correlated with children's abilities to use verb tenses correctly. My daughter did not understand "took" versus "taken" or when to use the suffix "-ed." She often asked why her stories had to have

"-ed" at the end of most of the verbs. She did not understand past tense versus present tense, let alone use of a past participle. As developmental changes advanced, her ability to grasp these concepts emerged. When she no longer asked but applied correct verb tenses, I was elated. But then she started asking about the past participle and how it is used in comparison to past tense. I found this amazing — something I thought she might never grasp.

As the following individual stories show, every child with neuro-developmental delay, in my experience, has also shown vestibular dysfunction in some way, and levels of severity vary. Every child has also shown maturity of the vestibular system through vestibular stimulation from early stages of development, stimulation of the primitive reflexes, or a combination of both.

Andrew

I met Andrew when he was eight years old, having been previously diagnosed with Sensory Processing Disorder, ADHD, Developmental Coordination Disorder and a learning disorder. He participated in occupational and speech therapies at age four. His mother said during birth he was briefly stuck in the canal, and just after birth he had heavy bruising on his right clavicle area and on the right side of his neck. He suffered numerous ear infections during his first year, broken eardrums twice, and finally had tubes put in his ears. Academically he was behind. His parents were concerned about his well-being socially, behaviorally, and academically. Andrew started NDD therapy with one vestibular exercise that varied slightly for a year.

During his first two months, he said the exercise felt

good and he thought he was running faster. School was stressful and emotions were high. In the next two months, he started riding a bike, climbing fences and trees, eating more, growing, and experiencing a slightly improved emotional state. That summer, eight months into NDD therapy, his mother said he showed remarkable improvement in coordination. Andrew was active in sports: soccer, biking, basketball, baseball, swimming. Schoolwork was still a struggle — reading and math were "challenging." Substantial academic improvements had apparently been observed, however, because the school called his mother and asked what Andrew had been doing. The next school year — nearly a year after starting NDD therapy — Andrew was active physically and reading had improved significantly, having become his strongest subject.

Jack

Jack, age 12 ½ , started NDD therapy with a vestibular exercise targeting early stages of normal development. He continued with the exercise for several months, and during that time his mother said she noticed improvements regarding impulsivity and overreactive behavior. "Calmer" was the word she repeated several times to describe the change. When he came to see me one day, six months after starting NDD therapy, his mother shared some paragraph writing Jack had completed using a specific homeschool curriculum. I was astounded by how well his paragraphs were organized and how well they showed sequencing of information. His mother said she, too, was surprised, particularly because just six months ago he had been unable to even understand the directions in the curriculum, let alone complete a writing assignment. I was convinced that major vestibular changes had taken place and began to retest specific areas. Eye convergence and eye tracking both showed significant improvement. I said, "Jack, what have you been up to regarding sports, or playing outside, or physical activities?" He thought and then exclaimed, "Oh, I know! I've been playing catch with a football and I'm much better at catching a ball." His mother agreed and then shared stories about how his social and relational skills had also improved. She said he had become confident and more aware of others' needs.

I think many children who struggle with body awareness and how their own bodies take up space and move in space also struggle with understanding how to relate or respond to others. Their own insecurities regarding body awareness lead to becoming overly focused on themselves. As this begins to stabilize — they fit inside their bodies better, begin to be able to adapt to others around them, and then become more able to recognize needs, body language, and the emotions of others. Jack is a good example of this pattern of growth.

Sandra

I met Sandra when she was almost six years old. Previous diagnoses included ADHD, speech delay, and sensory processing disorder. She had experienced extensive occupational and speech therapies, as well as visits with a neurological chiropractor and a psychologist. During the pregnancy, her mother experienced severe emotional stress from the death of a family member. Sandra was breech during the last three months of the pregnancy and delivered by caesarian section.

My first encounter with Sandra was a treat. She wore a tutu with leggings and danced around the room, often in her own little world. At other times, she engaged and interacted with me using body language more often than speech. Her parents had forewarned me she did not respond to questions unless with one-word answers, and she did not engage in conversation. Sandra took advantage of opportunities to tease. She called, "Help" when asked to get up off the floor, smiled mischievously and danced away from me when I attempted to approach, and lifted onto her tiptoes when I asked her to place her feet next to each other. It became evident she wanted her own way, but she demonstrated it in a very playful manner.

We started NDD therapy with one vestibular exercise that varied during the first several months; then we changed to a second vestibular exercise. Each of the exercises targeted stimulation from early stages of normal development. In the first few months, school remained a problem, as Sandra often wandered about and showed a lack of interest or ability to stay on task. Her parents pulled her from private school and began homeschooling. Within the first four months, Sandra had begun riding a bicycle and a scooter. Talking increased. She showed better interaction with other children and starting sharing her toys with friends. She started dressing herself. She began to read and was able to recall names of shapes.

Within the first ten months of NDD therapy, Sandra showed progress in reading. She had become quite a talker and was able to converse, her maturity had escalated, and she started playing with more advanced toys. Her mother shared with me as she wiped at her tears, "I'm so happy, and now I want more." A mother after my own heart.

When I met with Sandra's family 14 months after she started NDD therapy, we discussed her status. She continued to be overly sensitive to loud sounds such as in noisy restaurants and while watching fireworks. Her scalp was still tender and she disliked having her hair brushed. Her teeth were not as sensitive as they had been, and her mother said she had become more comfortable with brushing her teeth. Behavior was still fidgety at the dinner table; her mother said she ate better when being fed.

Her parents expressed delight, with her changes in speech. Sandra had progressed from saying only one word at a time to toddler speech, in which she omitted words such as "is," "has," and "was," but now spoke in complete sentences. She became more open to learning, more independent, and loved pretend play. Regarding school, Sandra continued to be easily distracted during school work and her mother found clever ways to redirect her to tasks at hand. At times, Sandra was quite calm and on task, and she accomplished a lot of work; at other times, she was more easily distracted and the school day progressed slowly. Her mother said she was amazed by Sandra's wonderful memory.

Sandra completed listening therapy a few months before her second anniversary of NDD therapy. Subtle changes in verbal expression such as describing her likes and dislikes were noticed. She began conversing with staff members in our office and with younger children. We were thrilled when she started spelling words by sound before completing the listening therapy.

To date, Sandra has matured to age-appropriate

levels in many areas, while other areas continue to show infant, toddler, and younger-child behavior. Yet, friends and relatives are regularly commenting that Sandra is maturing, speaking clearly, playing games with others — behaving more "normal." The progress continues, and her parents are grateful for what they have seen so far. Sandra's mother has shared that she is delighted to be on this journey of hope with her daughter.

Chapter 10

New Sounds, New Voices: The Role of Listening Therapy

While 100 percent of the children in NDD therapy have initially shown impaired eye movements (for reading, writing, near-to-far adjustments, etc.), most also show auditory processing difficulties. In normal development, the auditory system begins development at the same time as the vestibular, sensory, and tactile systems, and it continues to develop after the other systems have matured. A lack of full maturity in the earlier-developing systems may affect later development of the auditory system. Some children naturally show some auditory processing changes as they progress through NDD therapy; others show profound changes; and many need listening therapy to further stimulate development of the auditory system.

In early development, as the Moro Reflex withdraws, it triggers maturation of the stapedius muscle inside the ear. This muscle contracts and relaxes in response to loud and soft noises. Children with sound sensitivity may have underdeveloped functionality of the stapedius muscle, and children who are oversensitive to noise, in my experience, consistently show the continued presence of the Moro Reflex. As the reflex withdraws over time, sensitivity to noise generally improves. Some children show changes in the auditory system once the Moro Reflex initiates withdrawal. This is evident not only through noticeably diminished sensitivity to sound, but also through improvements in speech and articulation, the ability to follow directions, and occasionally working memory and processing speed. After several months of NDD therapy, if parents have not noticed significant changes in these areas, I reevaluate and typically find the children need listening therapy.

The First Half: The Receptive Phase

The listening therapy*, divided into two 30-hour phases, allows children to retrace development of listening from pre-birth through beginning speech, and into academic applications for those who are able and ready. The first half allows children to experience sound similarly to that of babies inside the womb. During the first 30 hours (which is typically further divided into two hours a day), children engage in quiet activities while listening to Mozart compositions and Gregorian chant on headphones. Mozart's music is used because the compositions include a broad range of frequencies. The individual hears filtered music that "comes and goes" (this is similar to how an infant hears sounds in the womb).

---

*Anna's House uses the Listening Fitness Program®, created by The Listening Centre, Toronto, Canada (www.listeningfitness.com).

Gradually, over several consecutive days, the lower frequencies are pulled out and higher and higher frequencies in the music are heard. By completion of the first 30 hours, children finally hear the music in all its fullness, just as a newborn hears sound in all its fullness.

Most parents describe small notable changes during the first half of the listening. One mother, an incredible observer, noticed significant changes in her son during the first half of his listening. His tone of voice changed more appropriately to given situations. He played with his voice, making random repetitive sounds ("waba, dada, baba"). He talked about hearing his mother's flip-flops on the carpet (sound-absorbent surfaces) instead of only when she walked across the kitchen floor. For the first time, he heard the kitchen oven turning off and on to maintain the temperature and door latches opening and closing. He heard the dog's tennis ball hit the floor, the sound of riffling papers, scissors cutting paper, feet tapping, the sounds of a computer keyboard when his mother typed — all for the first time. He told his mother he could hear spoons touching bowls for the first time and the sound made when paper towels are ripped apart. When he heard leaves rustling in the trees, he finally understood what his mother had meant when she said, "Listen to the leaves." He shared one day that he now knew the word "perfectly" was not "perPectly," as he had previously thought. He realized the store Vitamin Cottage was not Vitamin *College*. He heard words in songs more clearly.

Activities children engage in also show improvement. Some children start doing jigsaw puzzles for the first time; others are able to assemble Lego pieces into a specific object from following pictorial instructions. Some children begin to understand counting of spaces while playing board games, while others start to understand sequencing in games or directions or strategies. Many children develop artistic skills, and we see improvements in drawing and sketching. These changes suggest that maturity within the vestibular system is taking place.

Behaviors of individuals vary during the listening sessions. Some children curl up and sleep through much of it; others begin to play independently and quietly for the first time. Some become agitated and want to annoy others, while some start to engage with other children and share toys or activities. Many children play with their voices. In our office, we often notice signs of maturity as the children, teens, and young adults begin to walk more confidently, make better eye contact, greet staff warmly, and engage in or initiate conversation. While some parents notice improved ability to focus and stay on task with homework or at desks during school, other parents say they notice no changes whatsoever. When I hear this, I know the bulk of the changes for these children will come during or after the second half of the listening therapy.

The Second Half: The Expressive Phase

After a four-to-six week break, the second half introduces speech, beginning with sounds similar to that of a toddler and progressing according to the ability of each individual. Also 30 hours in length (divided into two hours a day), the second half first reintroduces the child to the range of frequencies via listening to the music, and then a microphone is added and speech activities engage. Sessions are divided between listening quietly and engaging in one-on-one activities. Children are challenged to listen to the voice of their instructor as well as their own voices, which is often a new experience. They are asked to separate sounds in words and syllables, carefully discriminate between sounds that are close in audible frequency, repeat directions verbatim, complete tasks in sequence, read aloud if applicable, and listen while being read to. Some also spell sound-by-sound and write from dictation. The auditory system is stimulated through speech and processing, and the changes have been remarkable.

Children have shown improved enunciation, increased vocabulary, improved articulation, and better control of the volume levels of their own voices. Depending on age and ability, children have consistently shown improvements in reading, spelling, and writing. Reading progress includes decoding, inflection, and comprehension. Spelling one-and two-syllable words and compound words by sound allows children to break visual spelling habits and typically leads to visual-auditory integration in reading, spelling, and writing.

Working Memory and Processing Speed

After the listening therapy, nearly every individual is given daily follow-up work for a time so that old habits and compensations can be put aside and natural patterns for reading, writing, and processing engage. Parents and teachers often notice changes in working memory or processing speed. Many times we see it begin prior to completion of the second half of the listening.

Working memory is retaining partial information and applying it to what comes next. An example in math might be (5+3) + 2. Working memory allows an individual to retain the sum of eight (5+3) and then add two. A child without working memory related to math would most likely forget the sum of eight and then lose the ability to solve the problem. A reading example might involve a multi-syllable word such as "recreation." While attempting to divide the word into syllables in order to decode the word, the child is unable to retain all of the individual syllables in order to put the entire word together. As a result, he or she might say something like "retion." I have witnessed astounding changes in children regarding reading of multi-syllable words during the second half of the listening therapy. This would naturally affect articulation, enunciation, verbal expression, reading, comprehension, writing (including sentence, paragraph, and multi-paragraph papers), homework, test taking, etc. Improvements in working memory affect processing speed.

Attention

Many children show improved attention and become less drawn away by distractions in the classroom. They are better able to tune into the sounds they need to hear and tune out background sounds. Prior to the listening therapy, these children commonly hear all sounds equally and are unable to ignore background noise. I remember one teenager told me his mother took him to the basement to do homeschooling because the ticking of a particular clock annoyed him severely. After NDD and the listening therapies, he no longer struggled with being able to tune out background sounds.

I participated in the listening therapy myself so that I would know what children experience. At the time, I attended an aerobics class at the nearby recreation center. I remember attending class and being frustrated with the loud music while at the same time trying to hear the instructor's verbal directions. Then one day I became suddenly aware that I could tune out the music and pull in the instructor's voice.

After completion of the listening therapy, some children, while able to hold attention, hang onto old habits. They appear to continue to struggle with staying on task in the classroom. In my experience, this usually indicates a need to cut back on screen time, turn off the TV, and hold the child accountable for his or her behavior. I often tell children that paying attention should no longer be a problem. It has become a choice.

Hearing One's Voice

A few adults have completed the listening therapy with their children. I have heard these parents' reading change from monotone to having good inflection. A mother realized as she better heard her own voice how much she actually yelled at her own children. Her tone and pitch changed for the better, and now she expresses her feelings with a monitored voice.

Both adults and children have changed the volume of their voices during and after the listening. Children with loud voices have been surprised to hear how loud their voices sound. Later, when a parent says, "Use your indoor voice," the children understand and are able to lower their voices. Other children have soft voices, and during and after the listening therapy their voices raise so they are better heard. My daughter's voice rose considerably. Every so often, I may say, "Speak up, I can't hear you," and she does. Before the listening therapy, she didn't know what I meant when I told her to speak up.

First-time Moments

Many children diagnosed with autism are described as children who do not ask about others, do not ask questions, or do not initiate words (they repeat words but do not say words on their own). It is not unusual to hear these children begin to ask questions during the listening therapy. Often, the questions have been about another child in listening therapy that might be absent that day. I remember a particular boy started asking about another boy who had become quite sick; each day he asked how the boy was and when he might come back. Soon he was asking about staff members, and his questions continued to broaden. Another boy, prior to the listening therapy, repeated simple words but did not initiate words on his own, and I was told he never asked questions. One day he finished his listening session and asked his mother, "What are we having for lunch?" During another session, this same boy repeated words in a book that I read to him. We did this several times using the same book. Then I pointed to a cow without saying anything and he said, "Moo." In cases like this, what seems to be a simple thing is actually a profound moment in a child's life.

I have witnessed first-hand moments of change in children. Something literally changes in the brain, and they suddenly respond differently. Some children start out slow to respond, hesitant, struggling with directions or with processing information. They may try and try and try, and yet the task seems overwhelming. Then, the next moment or the next day, something is different and the child "gets it." Even the children are aware of the change, and they are delighted. Response time is faster, processing is faster, and eagerness, desire, and motivation move into higher gear. The one-on-one sessions move to a new level.

New Abilities and Academic Growth

As children complete the listening therapy, I am most excited about what I see as new-found abilities. While some children and teens become much more verbally assertive and begin to show leadership abilities or speech and debate skills, others need to advance academically. The greatest hindrance has time and again been related to school demands. Organizationally, schools tend to not have the flexibility to allow children to work through the early stages of development before requiring specific academic achievements. While I show parents foundational tools for reading, spelling, writing, or math that will allow a child to catch up, schools typically require a child to be able to perform close to grade level or enter a special education program that has sometimes been counterproductive. In my experience, homeschooled children usually catch up at a significantly faster rate than children who attend school away from home. Not all homeschooled children progress at a rapid pace; every child is his or her own person and needs to move at his or her own pace. Even so, homeschooled children who learn slowly generally progress faster, over time, than similar children who attend a school because flexibility is available to move according to the children's needs.

I remember a teen who showed slight neuro-developmental delay and auditory processing difficulties. He completed NDD therapy in less than a year, which overlapped the listening therapy. As he completed the listening therapy, his ability to sequence and process information was much improved. He shared his anxieties about having to write essays, particularly on timed tests. He said he had never been able to do it and thought he never would. In the past, when he encountered a test question that asked for an essay answer, he would lay his pencil down and, as far as he was concerned, the test had ended. He needed to know that this should no longer be a problem. I spent three one-hour sessions with this young man, providing tools and practicing writing with him. Each time I sent home two or three assignments for him to work on independently. In less than two months he easily developed well-written essays in a short amount of time, and his confidence to be able to do it on tests was in place. His "final exam" with me was fascinating to observe. I gave an impromptu topic and asked him to develop his thoughts mentally, verbalize those thoughts in an organized manner, and then present an oral essay. He performed splendidly.

A young teen who attended a private school struggled academically and socially. He often refused to read or write, completion of homework was sporadic, and he suffered with tremendous developmental delay and auditory processing. Improvements came socially, behaviorally, and finally academically after he completed the listening therapy and near the end of NDD therapy. His teachers and parents noticed improved working memory and processing speed. I met with him for an hour each week for reading and writing practice.

What had been illegible writing became organized, well-developed paragraphs, and, for the first time, he showed pride in his work. I insisted on good enunciation while reading and we spent a lot of time reading to each other. Comprehension improved dramatically and his reading level climbed. We added math to our weekly meeting. His retention of information expanded and he no longer needed to relearn the same information each time he looked at fractions or multiplication facts or multi-digit subtraction problems.

Another teen, previously diagnosed with autism, started the listening after having begun NDD therapy over a year earlier. His mother said he read beginner books but used the words he chose rather than what was written, and he could not answer "why" questions after reading. During his listening therapy, he particularly liked to read Disney fairytale books aloud. He often merely told the story as he turned the pages. Actual reading did not take place, just as his mother had said. After starting the second half of listening, he began reading simple words and then simple sentences accurately. He then read some simple Dr. Seuss books and *Frog and Toad* books, receiving constant reminders to read exactly what was written. His comprehension, however, was based on his interpretation of the illustrations.

Casual conversation gradually increased and then he started to read Roald Dahl's book *Fantastic Mr. Fox*. Our entire office staff was thrilled when one day he retold what he had read accurately, and when asked how he thought the story might end, he actually thought about it and made suggestions. He began to answer "why" questions. For example, part way through the book he was asked who he thought was a mean character and why. He said the fox was mean because he stole chickens. After finishing the book, he was asked if it ended the way he thought it might. He responded no, and that he liked the book's ending better because, "No one got hurt and no one is hungry." These changes in reading took place within a three-week span.

Parents who see the least amount of change consistently share the same one or two problems. Either they were inconsistent or dropped the daily follow-up from the listening or they chose to use a curriculum other than what was recommended and then were disappointed. Many parents share my wish that academic catching up will come quickly and without hiccups. It does not happen with any child, let alone those who have been delayed. Personalities may be resistant, obstinate, impulsive, or a child may significantly struggle with one or two subjects, but the difference is that the behavior of a once-delayed child is typically more within the "normal" age-appropriate range.

> Many parents share my wish that academic catching up will come quickly and without hiccups. It does not happen with any child, let alone those who have been delayed.

Overall, for many, many children with neuro-developmental delay and auditory processing difficulties, academics do not begin to advance until after the listening therapy. For some, it is a giant step forward and a leap to the top; for others, the foundations of learning are just beginning. However a given child responds to the listening, progress is noted.

Chapter 11

The Tortoise Beats the Hare Again: The Long But Fruitful Road to Academic Growth

While NDD therapy has proven helpful for stimulating maturity of the central nervous system, it is not enough for most parents to end at that point. Parents like me want to see a difference in their child's academics. I desperately wanted my daughter to function as a whole person, and I would not have been satisfied if we had stopped once she began to function normally in day-to-day activities. I wanted her to be able to read and write and do general math. I wanted her to know about the world around her, about history and plants and the stars. I feel this way about the children I work with as well. I want more for them than maturity in the central nervous system. I want to see a difference in their academic performance. I want to know that a child can catch up in school.

Numerous children struggle with classroom situations as they participate in NDD therapy, whether in public, private, Montessori or charter schools. Expectations are beyond their scope for a time, which makes it difficult for classroom and special education teachers. The frustrations, in my opinion, come from a school's lack of being able to accommodate according to a child's needs during a time when he or she needs to be able to function at a lower age and grade level. Teachers are nearly always under specific standards imposed by school systems as a whole, and are often unable to accommodate in specific, individualized manners. Homeschooling allows parents this flexibility and does it quite successfully, in my experience. Although I have known a few children I have worked with who attend school and were able to catch up academically, those who are homeschooled generally catch up faster and more successfully.

Angela struggled through fourth grade in her private school and then struggled again through fifth grade. Suggestions were made for modifications to her school work, yet she was expected to perform at grade level. Her frustration showed in what I thought was depression and withdrawal. Lashing out at her siblings continued and she seemed like an angry young girl. Her grandparents, legal guardians of Angela and her siblings, decided to pull her out of school and started homeschooling. After the first month and a half, they were discouraged as Angela did not want to do her school work, threw temper tantrums, and behaved defiantly. Her grandparents and I met and reviewed her curriculum. We agreed that they would eliminate much of the paperwork as it was merely busy work. We also agreed to try a different approach to reading, writing, and spelling and relied on more videos and projects in science and social studies/history with less textbook reading. Instead of using a traditional math textbook, they approached math developmentally. She started with daily review of math facts and reading multi-digit numbers so that understanding place value became secure. Within two months she started rounding multi-digit numbers and counting money using dimes and pennies.

Her grandparents set aside time daily to read to Angela and to listen to her read to them. At our next visit, they were elated with Angela's attitude toward school. She was retaining what she learned, applying herself, enjoying school, progressing in each subject, and behaving better. She looked happier than I had ever seen. A former teacher of Angela's shared that she noticed a happier girl with a new interest in learning. Her progress continued such that I enjoyed reading her well-written, multi-paragraph papers.

I remember a boy who had been previously diagnosed with PDD (Pervasive Developmental Delay) and high-functioning autism. He started NDD therapy when he was about seven-and-a-half. A year and a half later, his school expressed they were no longer concerned about his behavior; they were trying to ascertain how best to help him academically. At the same time, his parents were frustrated because they worked with their son at home with reading and writing techniques we use at *Anna's House*, and their son performed at a much higher level at home than at school.

Another young man, now 18, first came to see me when he was 13. When I met him, his eye contact was nonexistent and he talked to his mother, but not to me. Not only did he not make eye contact, his eyes did not converge at all, so reading was extremely difficult. His speech was severely impaired and I struggled to understand anything he said. As he worked through NDD therapy, listening therapy, and finally academic tutoring, he developed maturity in the central nervous system. We became good friends as he grew to welcome the world around him. Conversation became easy and he was popular amongst his peers in high school. Speech, although still impaired, improved. He started to read simple words by sound rather than recalling the few he had memorized. By the time he was 18, his reading and comprehension reached third-grade level and his school was delighted with his progress. When he graduated from high school, his parents were told that his reading would never improve beyond his current level. He and I continued to meet for tutoring, but only one hour every other week. In less than six months following his graduation, he advanced another two grade levels in reading and comprehension. He and his parents refuse to give up and I applaud and support their determination.

As children near completion of NDD therapy, we work with many academically in order to help them catch up. While some of these children attend public or private school, others are homeschooled. Several homeschooling families meet with us periodically for assistance or coaching as they work hard to help their children excel. Many hours have been spent coaching parents about particular subjects, and sometimes we teach a child a particular lesson while the parents observe. Occasionally, parents need suggestions, but most of the time they just need a bit of encouragement.

Reading

When a child's reading is poor or even nonexistent, and if he or she shows developmental delay, I encourage parents to put it on the back burner for a time. If a school-age child manifests behaviors of a much younger child, perhaps toddler-age or even infantile, the push for reading creates frustration for parents, teachers, and especially the child. Lack of good eye convergence and/or eye tracking is nearly always part of the problem. The child is physiologically not ready for reading. The best thing parents can do in this situation is read to their child — often. Professionals agree that parents should read to their infants, toddlers, and preschool children, and this is similarly a critical part of helping an older child who may continue to be "stuck" in earlier stages of development.

Reading aloud to children of any age provides innumerable benefits. Young children and children with developmental delay can learn from listening to their parents read. They hear inflection, sentence structure, complete sentences, and how a voice reads text. Visualization and imagination are stirred and encouraged. They hear for themselves the enjoyment of reading. Reading is a precursor to writing, and a necessary part of a developmentally delayed child's day. Just as parents are routinely encouraged to read aloud to their children, I habitually encourage parents to read aloud to their delayed children at lower levels and then advance as the children are ready.

When a child begins to show a desire for reading, I typically find that eye movement changes have substantially improved and at least some of the primitive reflexes have withdrawn considerably. Unless the child also shows significant auditory processing difficulties, now is the time to start the child reading. Children who learn to read sound-by-sound instead of visually memorizing words, guessing, or reading by the context of sentences become far better readers than their peers. I have seen this again and again. I encourage parents to teach reading sound-by-sound and follow it with spelling by sound and verbal dictation. The child then reads from his own writing what was dictated. Accurate reading leads to more advanced reading and better comprehension.

I remember a teen who, in my opinion, was a poor reader and speller. His school report said his reading was at grade level but his comprehension was quite low. When he read aloud to me, he often misread words. For example, in a given passage he read the word "mare" and when I asked him what it meant, he said, "A guy who runs a town" — thinking it was a mayor. This teen's problem was not comprehension, but accurate reading (decoding). As we worked through tutoring sessions, his reading, writing, and spelling improved and he no longer required a special education program at school.

A child with significant auditory processing difficulties often is not ready to read until after completing the listening therapy. When sound discrimination improves and the child is better able to separate and identify given sounds in words, the child has usually reached reading-readiness. By this time, the primitive reflexes have shown substantial withdrawal, eye movements have improved, and the child should be ready to begin a reading program. While some children advance quickly and their reading rapidly climbs, others show slow yet steady progress.

Frustration comes when a school program or a specific curriculum does not adapt or work with children based on developmental stages of growth. Parents sometimes hope their children will suddenly or magically begin to read independently. Some children take off like a rocket, and others need the next step — good tutoring based on developmental growth and reading based on sound. The children who come to our office for reading assistance as follow-up to the listening therapy have consistently shown tremendous gains, some faster than others.

When a child begins to read, she must first know the sounds of the alphabet. Reading is a process of blending sounds and parents must insist their children sound out words as they read. *Anna's House* often starts a child reading two- and three-letter words written on index cards. In some cases, a group of cards can be laid across the floor or on a table in order to make a simple sentence. Some parents include *Bob* books and other beginner reader books. I have found that progression typically moves from reading words on index cards to spelling those same words, to dictation of sentences using the same words, to having the child read aloud the sentences she completed from dictation, to reading books. Some children start with simple beginner books. At *Anna's House*, we start many new readers with *Dragon Slayer's Academy* books. I like this series because the bulk of the words are phonetically based for ease of sounding out, and character names are consistent with phonetic rules. I have seen young children develop a love of reading from this point and I have seen 15-year-olds ask to read more books in the series. Most other books, even beginner reading material, often include words that cannot be sounded out, and names are often very difficult to decipher. At *Anna's House*, children of all ages usually follow this or a similar procedure and then advance to higher and higher levels rather quickly. Most of these children spend 30 or more minutes at one time reading aloud. Inflection, enunciation, accurate reading, sounding out words, and discussion are all required.

Teens can also catch up from low levels of reading. My daughter advanced from reading at a third-grade level at age 18 to reading adult books by age 21. As much as I wanted to be the one to tutor her, she worked better when I hired someone to use my curriculum, and she caught up. At *Anna's House*, we have observed both children and teens progress in reading regardless of age or how far behind they were when we started.

Homeschooling mothers often worry about their children's progress when delay is involved. It is common for homeschooling mothers to compare themselves and their children to other homeschoolers. I did it, and I encourage parents to not do this. Parents often repeatedly ask over the course of several months, "Are you sure it's okay to wait longer for reading?" And when the child is finally ready, the parents are relieved. The parents who wait until their children are developmentally ready typically see faster gains than those whose children who have previously learned and implemented reading compensation skills.

There are some children who progress slowly and their parents find it discouraging. One boy still was not reading at age ten. When he reached the point in NDD therapy in which the primitive reflexes showed substantial inhibition, eye movements were smooth, and the listening therapy was complete, I encouraged his parents to start the reading curriculum we use as part of his homeschooling. A year later, his mother was nearly in tears in my office because her son's reading continued to be painfully slow. As I talked with the family, I observed that the boy struggled with extreme anxiety about reading. He did not show anxiety about anything else we discussed — only reading. He spoke confidently and with good eye contact about a variety of subjects, but as soon as the topic of reading came up, he stuttered and hesitated, fidgeted, and dropped eye contact. In this case, the best thing the parents could do was let go of their own anxieties about their son's reading. Once this boy's parents released their anxiety, their son began reading and enjoying it. Children pick up on their parents' anxieties and often manifest their parents' emotions through their own behavior. When I stopped stressing about my daughter's progress and accepted each step for what it was, the dynamics of everything improved. I was more relaxed, she became more relaxed; I stopped worrying about her academic levels, and she approached academics more willingly; I stopped fretting over childish behavior, and she readily took on more responsibilities.

Children who attend school away from home generally are significantly slower with progress in reading. This is not always the case, but I am not surprised when I hear that it is. I remember one family whose daughter's reading was several grades below level. She showed neuro-developmental delay and impaired eye movements. When she completed NDD therapy and her eye movements were smooth, her parents were frustrated that she was still well below grade level in reading. At the same time, the school pushed for testing for special education. I assured them that the physiological hindrances to reading were no longer present and with good tutoring she should catch up without difficulty. For most children, reading does not magically appear once physiological developmental delays have resolved.

Parents with patience are a blessing to their children.

Many parents willingly yield to whatever level their children manifest, patiently work with them through NDD therapy, and in most cases, the listening therapy,

Parents with patience are a blessing to their children.

and then (for those who homeschool) just as patiently begin or change their schooling program. These parents applaud their children's progress, whatever the pace, and focus on the positive, encouraging changes. Across the board, these children progress through the entire process the smoothest and with the greatest stability.

Spelling

Reading and spelling go hand-in-hand. The way in which a child reads is often the way in which he also spells and writes. Children who struggle with reading and spelling often show dyslexic-type symptoms or spell "phonetically," such as using just "r" instead of "er." While this is commonly referred to as phonetic spelling, in actuality it is spelling by sound without use of phonetic principles. When reading or spelling, they may reverse or transpose letters, omit letters in blends, randomly choose vowels, and omit or change suffixes. Each time I have seen one or more of these, I have also found a continued presence of the primitive reflexes at the brain stem level as well as auditory processing difficulties. Discrimination of sounds is nearly always negligible in these children. They often show confusion of middle and ending sounds in words when listening and repeating words. As these same children progress through NDD therapy and then complete the listening therapy, they begin to apply sound to spelling while learning basic phonetic rules of spelling at the same time. Some children grasp it quickly, others slowly, but spelling improves.

Many children show good spelling while we work with them, but then their spelling scores in school remain low. I remember one nine-year-old girl whose spelling was significantly below grade level. As I showed her how to spell by sound during her listening therapy, her spelling improved dramatically. I sent word lists home for her to practice reading and spelling during the remainder of the summer months. Once she started back to school, her spelling deteriorated. Her parents and I continued with spelling lists outside of school and were thrilled to see that her spelling when writing improved, although scores on spelling tests did not.

I often see weekly spelling lists that are random with regard to phonics. Many lists include multiple spelling variations of a particular vowel sound. For example, I have seen many spelling lists that incorporate multiple spellings for the sound of long "a": pain, pay, eight, vein, plate, prey. This confuses and frustrates some children so that memorizing each word is their only solution. It would be better if the spelling list contained words with the long "a" sound but used only one of the several spellings, such as "ai." The children can practice listening to the sounds, for example, in the word "pain" and break the word into its individual sounds while knowing that the long "a" sound will be spelled with "ai." This allows visual and auditory integration to take place — seeing a word and listening to the sounds in the word.

Spelling curriculums usually require children to write the words a certain number of times and complete other activities that all require memorization. Spelling, however, should not be memorized except when words or specific syllables show atypical spelling and phonetics do not apply. If a child is able to discriminate individual sounds in words, and learns to spell with word lists that can all be spelled by sound instead of memorized, then spelling in writing shows better accuracy. I have given children word lists that, for example, consist of the short "a" sound. One and two-syllable words, a few three-syllable words, and compound words were all part of the list, but the short vowel rules applied to every word on the list (as well as every syllable in each of the words), and memorization was not required. It becomes a process of implementation of sound-to-spelling. Later, when the child writes sentences or a paragraph with words from the same word lists, good spelling can be expected.

When *Anna's House* assists homeschool families with reading and spelling, we do not provide weekly lists for tests. The children read and spell from dictation according to a stated phonetic sound, rule, or application. As we dictate from the given word list, we log a cumulative list of misspelled words. Sentences using the words from the list are dictated and we make note of the spelling errors within given sentences. The child is encouraged to find and correct all errors, we discuss misspelled words, and the child corrects each mistake. On another day, we tell the child we are having a review and we dictate only the words from the cumulative word log. By this time, the child should be able to spell the words with good accuracy. If not, we review the lesson again until the child has grasped it, and then move on. Not only does the child show good spelling, but he has shown that he can apply correct spelling when writing. Evidence of good spelling

> Evidence of good spelling shows in writing.

shows in writing.

Writing

Reading and spelling go hand-in-hand, and writing is closely tied to both. Children write based on how they read. For example, those who write run-on sentences, read in run-on fashion. Some parents have argued this with me when we study their children's written work, but each time we listen together as their child reads aloud, the child reads the same way in which he writes sentences — usually in run-ons. Many of them are good readers, but the run-ons are there nonetheless. When the reading slows down and appropriate pauses develop, run-ons in writing cease.

Writing difficulties may be linked to developmental delay and/or auditory processing difficulties. Such children typically do not show improvement in writing until they have completed or nearly completed NDD and the listening therapies. Because writing skills can be affected by impaired eye movements, the continued presence of primitive reflexes, posture, vestibular function, and auditory processing, many children are not truly ready to write until many of these things are in place or nearly in place.

Dictation of sentences allows one to see how well children can copy what they hear. While some children need to hear just one or two words at a time in order to accurately write every word in a given sentence, others can handle large phrases. I am able to note a child's progress as he moves from hearing and accurately writing perhaps two words at a time, to four, to phrases, to sentences.

During the beginning stages of paragraph writing,

the instructor writes each sentence on a white board instead of the child, because at this point the goal is to stimulate the child's thinking and creativity without simultaneously pushing for writing skills. Developmentally, creative thinking comes prior to writing and, in this area as in all others, the desire is to closely follow natural patterns of development.

Paragraph development starts with writing as a team. At *Anna's House*, we may assign or ask the child for a topic, and then ask for one idea about the topic. Then we probe for a second idea, and then a third. Next, we have the child verbalize a sentence about the first idea, and we may push and pull for more details or more information. We may have to help so that we have a complete sentence. After writing one sentence for each of the three ideas, the instructor or the child reads the three sentences. We then help the child come up with a topic sentence and a closing sentence and then ask the child to copy the paragraph. This procedure is carried out over and over until the child knows the procedure and is able to do it independently.

As children are ready, they begin to develop paragraphs on their own, with guidance as needed, and ultimately, multi-paragraph papers. When we work with children one-on-one, we insist that all errors be corrected, and when the paper is finished, we applaud and praise a "perfect" paper. Time and again I have seen children who once hated writing develop a love for it. I often hear that writing used to be their worst subject and became their favorite. Not every child becomes a talented writer, but many parents are surprised at how well their children begin to write. Many teachers and special education teachers have applied this developmental writing technique to assist struggling children, and together we have rejoiced at the astounding progress.

Handwriting

The ability to shape letters correctly, grip a pencil, and recognize letters by sound in order to write them are precursors to writing. Children who have shown a Palmar Reflex often benefit by repeating phases of development related to pencil grip. These children usually benefit most by starting out with a thick, bullet-point marker and a whiteboard. This allows the pencil grip to mature naturally. As the hand, arm, and shoulder relax and the grip becomes more natural, the child then uses a thin marker on a whiteboard. The use of a whiteboard allows for easy erasures and freedom from concern about letter and word spacing or use of a baseline. As the child shows readiness and letter spacing is appropriate, we typically change to a lined whiteboard and start showing the child how to shape the letters appropriately using the top, middle, and baseline. We insist the child use her finger as a word-space guide; or if the child refuses, the instructor's finger becomes the word-space guide. Children gradually graduate from thin markers to fat pencils to regular-size pencils, and from whiteboards to wide, three-line paper, and then to narrower three-line paper.

I worked with one boy who showed a strong Palmar Reflex. As it inhibited, his school occupational therapist started pushing for school intervention regarding fine motor skills, yet the proposed approach was counterproductive to the natural pattern of development. The boy's mother described to the teacher how she wanted the school intervention to proceed: "We want you to start off by checking to see if he still has skills to master at the preschool/kindergarten level and, once each grade's skills have been mastered, then he can move up to the next grade's skill, etc., but do not leapfrog ahead." This mother was right. Her son needed the opportunity to retrace natural development once the reflexes withdrew.

Handwriting may improve and a child may demonstrate increased endurance if he does not have to sit on a chair at a desk, due to the continued presence of reflexes that impact posture. Or, one or more uninhibited reflexes may contribute to impaired eye tracking and hand-eye tracking so the parents may prefer to have the child practice shaping numbers and letters without concern just yet regarding letter spacing or writing on a base line.

One nine-year-old boy I worked with had shown tremendous developmental changes and maturity socially, behaviorally, and academically. Professionals at his school voiced concern about what they saw as a need for intervention with regard to his handwriting. They said he was slow completing writing assignments and his pencil grip was still awkward. I met with the boy and his mother in an effort to determine the root of the problem. I gave the boy an unlined whiteboard and exchanged thin markers for fat ones. As he wrote, I watched his posture, his writing arm (shoulder, elbow, wrist, hand, and grip), and then his writing. I discovered several interesting things. His letter shapes were drawn as individual art projects. When he drew a lower case "a," he drew around and around and around, and then made the descending line. Other letters, likewise, were shaped in complicated ways so that it was no wonder he was slow at writing. His grip was immature, but not incorrect. Since this boy had experienced neuro-developmental delay and impaired eye movements up through most of third grade, he had never had the opportunity to learn how to correctly shape letters of the alphabet. His mother and I agreed that he was ready to learn to shape letters using a lined white board, write with a thick marker for the time being, and that he should be supervised every time he practiced writing. Within just a few months, he progressed rapidly and was able to write comfortably and neatly on lined paper with a regular pencil.

Math

Just as with other academic skills, math can be impaired when a child is developmentally delayed. Occasionally, I have heard of and observed progress in math that occurs within the first several months of NDD therapy. For others, it does not improve until after completion of the program. I have noticed changes in math for many children when their vestibular system shows improved stability. When I hear that a child has shown improvements in math early on in NDD therapy, I have consistently found that the Moro Reflex showed inhibition at the same time. If a child who struggles in math does not show improved math skills within the first several months of NDD therapy, then I suggest to parents that it will most likely not come until the end, or after the child completes the therapy.

In my experience, many areas of struggle in math are related to vestibular function; these include comprehension of general mathematic concepts, place value, inverse operations such as addition versus subtraction, counting money, and learning to tell time. As children progress through NDD therapy and the vestibular system shows improved stability, changes are often reflected in math skills. I remember one ten-year-old girl who completed NDD and the listening therapies, and, as her fourth-grade school year ended, her teacher gave her mother math materials for the girl to complete during the summer in hopes of catching up just a little (she tested at first-grade level). I worked with this girl for several weeks during the summer and explained to her mother that instead of using the material provided by the school (two-digit addition and subtraction and learning multiplication and division), my desire was to start with basic math facts and place value. The approach was based on developmental growth instead of grade-level expectations. During the few weeks we met, this girl advanced from single-digit addition to multi-digit addition and subtraction, with carrying and borrowing. Her addition and subtraction skills advanced from first grade to fifth grade in a matter of weeks. She became excited about math and decided, for the first time, that she liked math. She had also begun to count money using dimes and pennies (tens and ones). Needless to say, her parents were ecstatic.

As the primitive reflexes withdraw and vestibular stability is demonstrated, changes in children's abilities to count money and transition between coin values generally improves. I remember my daughter was able to count dimes, but as soon as I added a penny or a nickel, she did not know what to do. After she completed NDD and the listening therapies, she began counting dimes and pennies correctly, since she now understood place value with tens and ones. When she became proficient at variations of adding and subtracting with dimes and pennies, I added nickels, then quarters, and finally dollars. She then wanted to be the banker when playing board games involving money. She started counting out money on her own when purchasing items at stores. This progressed to her desire for a bank account of her own, her own checkbook, and then her own debit card. She still gets excited (and so do I!) about being able to balance her checkbook without any help.

As children near completion of NDD therapy, those who struggled with being able to tell time generally start to show readiness as a result of changes in vestibular function. When children can spatially turn a clock around and know where the numbers should be, I then encourage parents to begin the process teaching time using clocks. I draw an imaginary clock on a wall and ask the child to point to where the quarter numbers should be (3, 6, 9, 12). Once they know this confidently, I pretend to pull the clock off the wall and "hold it" so that the imaginary clock is suspended in air, facing the child. He again points to the quarter numbers. When the child is able to note all the number locations correctly, I then turn the clock around so that the child is "behind" it and the clock faces away from the child. I again ask him to point to the quarter numbers and eventually all the numbers on the clock. In my experience, once this is successfully demonstrated, the child is ready to learn to read an analog clock, starting with just the hour hand.

Once basic math skills develop, later math skills follow. I often remind parents that this does not necessarily indicate their children will become gifted in math. Some need a math tutor for a while, and for some math continues to be a difficult subject. Few people excel in every subject and most of us can point out exactly which subject(s) we struggled with in school. Math is difficult for many.

Reading, spelling, writing, and math affect other subjects, so naturally weakness in any of these areas can and usually does affect other subjects. Every subject requires reading, most require writing, and some also require math skills. I have observed that as children complete NDD therapy (and possibly the listening therapy) they are usually better able to understand the concept of time — not just when reading a clock, but also in categorization of time periods, such as ancient history versus the Renaissance period versus recent history. My daughter showed amazing improvements with regard to understanding periods of time in history.

What I see again and again is that when signs of neuro-developmental delay are evident, and academic struggles are part of the problem, children cannot and should not be pushed to perform at higher levels prematurely. This is counterproductive. It also reinforces the idea that they think they are stupid or that something is wrong with them. Later, as academics begin to come together because they are physiologically ready, their attitudes and motivations typically show a desire to learn as well as excitement about their abilities. I consistently see children catch up and even exceed grade level. I think we all want children to develop a love of learning, as most of us spend our entire lives learning in one way or another.

Chapter 12

Progress Inhibitors

NDD therapy stimulates the central nervous system in a subtle, noninvasive manner. The entire program typically takes 18-24 months. A few children complete it in a about a year, while more severe cases may continue three years or longer. Several conditions, however, may slow or disrupt a child's progress. Simultaneous interventions, medications, the health of the child, consistency and commitment to the therapy, stresses of daily life, and stability in the home are all concerning factors. After a long period of accommodating and treating their child specially, parents who see the most gains are those who change with their child and raise expectations as the child is ready.

One Thing at a Time

NDD therapy is not a conglomeration of therapies. In fact, I have found through experience that when other interventions or therapies coincide with NDD therapy, little or no progress at the brain stem level is achieved. In the past, a few children I worked with demonstrated a puzzling lack of progress. Further inquiry revealed their parents had the children participating in occupational therapy, laser treatments, or other therapies at the same time. In each case, once the parents decided to at least temporarily end simultaneous interventions, progress resumed. NDD therapy stimulates natural development beginning at the brain stem. Simultaneous therapies seem to either overstimulate or prohibit changes at the brain stem level, preventing the children from making progress. This parallels normal development. We would never attempt multiple therapies with a newborn or toddler — one therapy to stimulate speech, another to stimulate walking, and another to target cognitive reasoning, while simultaneously encouraging tummy time.

In normal development, one thing naturally leads to another. When we target brain stem maturation, an individual needs time to let it develop and stimulate later abilities that lead to social, behavioral, and academic maturity. I frequently meet children who have been through multiple therapies prior to my acquaintance and yet still show underlying difficulties. These same children have shown substantial maturation after NDD therapy so that many no longer test as needing multiple therapies — some need no further intervention at all. Maturation of the central nervous system has done its work.

Medications

A child on psychotropic medications for behavior such as ADD/ADHD invariably shows extremely slow or no results with NDD therapy. I have worked with such children and observed that when they come off their medications during summer months, they make progress with NDD therapy. If they start back on the medications the following school year, NDD progress nearly halts until the following summer when they again break from taking their medications. Some children are able to wean off their medications prior to starting the therapy, and others gradually wean as they are able.

Potentially just as problematic, specific medications used by parents must be considered. I have worked with families in which a child showed sudden, unpredictable, emotional upheaval. I soon learned the mother or father had been on medications that were recently altered, which then affected the emotional stability of the parent. Some children mimic fears and anxieties they see exhibited in their parents and others become overly emotional when a parent is behaving "differently." I have come to suggest that a child's NDD therapy be put on hold for a time in these situations.

General Health

A few children suffer from significant health issues. Immunity might be greatly compromised and fluctuate so that progress with NDD therapy slows tremendously. An injury or major illness during NDD therapy may also slow the process. I remember one season in particular in which I encountered child after child who suffered a concussion and their therapy was put on hold for a few months. A broken bone may interfere with the ability of a child to participate in his or her given exercise for a time. In some cases, severe illness, surgeries, or hospital stays have interrupted the commitment for an extended period of time. Overall health prior to and during NDD therapy contributes to the duration of a child's program.

Consistency and Commitment

Yet another potential complication regarding the

success of NDD therapy is inconsistency with the given daily exercise. Consistency plays a significant factor toward the overall success of the program, which typically requires less than ten minutes each day. I remember one boy in particular whose parents were consistently hit-and-miss with the exercise. What should have been an 18-month program took nearly five years.

Both parents must be on board for this to be most successful. One parent should not be expected to carry the responsibility of NDD therapy with a child without the support of the other parent. Many times, relatives and extended family are not supportive, making it all the more important for both parents to support each other as well as their child. Many families have helped their children through the process while teachers, friends, and relatives voice their lack of support, and the children have progressed beautifully. As long as both parents work together to help their children, the process, while lonely, can still be successful. Some children go back and forth between their divorced parents' homes several times a week or month and the home life in each place may be drastically different. Both homes must be on board with NDD therapy in order for it to be most effective.

Stress

High stress environments stir up the emotions and then slow down the success rate. I have seen dramatic growth in several children until stress in the home affected their progress. One or both parents may be stressed about finances, job situations, relational conflicts, or any other number of possible stressors and these things can affect their children's behavior and emotions. Children are able to read their parents' emotions and often demonstrate erratic behavior when they sense stress in one or both parents.

Children often emulate one or both parent's emotions. I remember a mother called our office one day, emotionally upset with general daily stresses. She vented by screaming and yelling into the phone. Her chief complaint at the moment was that her son would not stop screaming and yelling. She later commented that when she slowed down on a given day and relaxed with her son, cuddling and reading with him, his behavior likewise was calm, relaxed and affectionate. This boy consistently mirrored his mother's emotions. I see this frequently.

> Children often emulate one or both parent's emotions.

Loss of a Loved One

Emotional upheaval may also occur with the death of a loved one, such as a grandparent. I have worked with children who suddenly and unexpectedly lost a grandparent or parent. This is traumatic and NDD therapy is most definitely affected. I have not seen regression, but I have seen some slowing down for a while.

Divorce or parent separation can be traumatic for children. Their grief and pain may be as intense as the death of a loved one. I have worked with families in which the parents separate or are newly divorced, and the child's therapy plateaus for a time.

Stability in the Home

In my experience, the more stable the home life, the

more smoothly a child progresses. Numerous times, I have noticed the emotional component of a child's progress follows the general emotional state of one or both parents. This is not always the case, but I have seen situations in which a calm parent who takes things in stride without being easily ruffled has a child who shows less emotional upheaval throughout NDD therapy than might typically be the case. A parent who tends to be more high-strung and easily moved emotionally may have a child who "bounces" emotionally for a longer period of time.

Raising the Bar

One of the most concerning situations I have experienced is how parents handle increased maturity in children who were initially severely delayed. As the children mature and move toward more age-appropriate behavior, their parents are often not sure what comes next. Discipline, day-to-day activities, and expectations must change, and many parents struggle with knowing how to move with their children. Parents and children have grown accustomed to allowances and other habits that may no longer necessarily apply. It is not unusual for me to hear that parents enroll in parenting classes or read parenting books in order to be able to change their approach toward their child. I used to protect my daughter when in public, especially when others approached her. When she matured and no longer required my intervention, I had to learn to stop it and keep my mouth shut. I had to change levels of expectations and hold her accountable for appropriate behavior. For many parents like me, it starts with treating children according to the age of their behavior. As they mature, this process continues until they reach their physical age. This process of moving with our children is more complicated in practice than in theory, but without these changes, children may not truly achieve their full potential.

Chapter 13

Teens and NDD Therapy:
Understanding Developmental Age

Parents of teenagers often notice up-and-down behaviors, similar to that of younger children. While it may be more agonizing for parents when the children are physically older, the process is much the same as that of younger children.

I remember the mother of a 16-year-old shared that during her son's first month of NDD therapy, she observed varied behavior. While he had begun to think of others in the family instead of just himself, he also showed increased selfish behavior. For example, he volunteered to cook dinner for the family (a first), but later spoke rudely to his mother. One moment she was surprised when he apologized for his rude behavior and demonstrated consideration for her and others, and the next moment he attempted to defy her authority. I often hear about teenagers yelling at their parents one moment and apologizing and seeking hugs the next. The teen has begun to recognize and acknowledge his or her inappropriate behavior. Over time, the behavior usually becomes more even-keeled and the extremes subside.

Verbal Expression

Other teens start NDD therapy as withdrawn individuals. Their parents have no idea what goes on inside their minds and desperately want to be able to connect. As teens work through inhibition of the Moro Reflex, they often initiate negative verbal expression that astounds their parents. I frequently notice teens who may routinely have nothing to say when they come to visit me one day walk into my office and literally tell me what they think about the therapy, their family, and the world. The parents are usually horrified and immediately demand an apology. I am thrilled, however, because I know this young person has just crossed a threshold developmentally. Verbal expression has begun!

As teens begin to express themselves for the first time, they often have to be taught appropriate forms of self-expression, just as with toddlers when they begin to verbalize. This normal pattern of development is retraced in older children, and even teens, when they begin to express themselves. I had to do this with my own daughter. At age 20, she needed guidance about how to appropriately express her feelings. I gave her "rules" regarding unacceptable words such as "hate" and often said, "If you feel this way, here is how you appropriately say it...." Verbal inappropriateness is more noticeable in a teen because parents assume they should already know this.

Parents often describe new occurrences of verbal lashing out, such as: "This exercise isn't helping me. I don't trust what it's doing. I don't trust you as my parents." My daughter, and many other teens, started out unable to recognize their own deficiencies. I reminded my daughter that I am her mother and she would continue with the exercise because we had made a commitment to seeing it through. No options. She was given spelled-out boundaries of acceptable versus unacceptable behavior and verbal language, just as parents do with toddlers. My daughter did not cross the line. I encourage other parents to follow through with predetermined consequences if their teens cross a stated line of acceptable behavior and language.

Verbal expression develops as socialization begins in normal development. As my daughter shared a desire for interaction with others, such as at church, I asked her to name one person she wanted to get to know. Then I gave her three questions to go ask the individual and instructed her to later share with me the answers to those questions. The following week I gave her two or three new questions to ask. Over time, this taught her how to engage socially with others, the value of showing an interest in others, and how to be a listener. I did not want her to think socialization is a process of others to talk about oneself. If we think about the age during which natural self-expression typically develops and what we do as parents with three-year-olds, it becomes less difficult to conceptually understand and help teenagers develop appropriate self-expression.

Cues for Assistance

As teens in particular mature through NDD therapy, parents are usually anxious to observe more age-appropriate behaviors. The teen years are hard enough without having delays in development. Parents often struggle with knowing when to "help" and when to back off. I remember a 15-year-old young man whose parents complained that he frequently objected to eating at fast-food places or even nice restaurants. Their son explained to me that a fast-food place in which he had to move through a line and make instant decisions about what he wanted on his sandwich was overwhelming and too fast for him. Likewise, eating at a restaurant that provided a large menu selection was overwhelming. While his parents struggled with comprehending this problem, I remembered my daughter had experienced the same difficulty. This is a common problem with those who show developmental delay, and most obvious in older children and teens. I suggested to the teen that when his family entered a place in which he felt overwhelmed in any way, he should discreetly tell one or both parents that

> Parents can partner with their teens using designated cues in specific situations until the teens are ready to take it on their own.

he would like help. His parents then stepped in and suggested maybe ordering for him as they proceeded through the line or, at a larger restaurant, asked what he might be in the mood for and directed him to one specific section of the menu. I found that when my daughter and I worked out this agreement, she was immediately more comfortable and no longer concerned about embarrassment. I found ways to protect her from humiliation and acted, as soon as I received the cue from her without challenging her expressed need. Parents can partner with their teens using designated cues in specific situations until the teens are ready to take it on their own.

Intuitiveness

Another aspect of maturity, most notable in teens because we naturally expect more mature behavior and responses from them than from younger children, is intuitiveness. I noticed that my daughter, just as always, did not naturally respond intuitively to situations after completing NDD therapy. At first I was frustrated because I wanted the intuition to be there, but then I learned how to work with it. I found that if I stopped what I was doing and explained what I wanted from her, she understood, responded appropriately, and applied it to future situations as well. For example, we carpool to the office each day and usually we carry armloads of various things to the car. Every morning for quite some time, I had to ask her to move so that I could open the back door of the car. It was the same thing every day — she would stand next to the car door and wait for me to open the door, but every day she stood blocking the door. Finally one day I explained that she was blocking the door and if she stepped back just one or two steps I could easily open the door without having to ask her to move. It never happened again! I learned that she may not have naturally or instinctively picked up on specific things, but when I explained, she got it. Prior to NDD therapy, I had explained and attempted to teach things like this and she just could not understand or "get it."

I noticed similar things when my daughter started cooking and balancing her checkbook. What used to be impossible to show, explain, or teach, became quickly learned. One day she showed me her checkbook, wondering about two checks that had not yet cleared the bank. I explained that if she added those two checks to her checkbook balance, the total should match her bank balance. She understood what I said the first time! I was flabbergasted. I did not have to explain it over and over and still see the blank look on her face. Parents may easily forget that we need to teach and explain things our teens missed along the way because they were delayed during the time in which they would have been expected to learn these things.

A few months after one young teen finished NDD

therapy, her mother complained that she was embarrassed when her daughter stared and pointed at a handicapped person they encountered. She had expected more mature behavior from her teen. We talked about the need to explain to her daughter the behavior that should have been demonstrated. This is commonly the case — what once was impossible to teach has become teachable. We as parents cannot expect behaviors to become innate when delay has been there, and it is exciting to find that we reach the point in which we can guide and teach our teens, and they get it!

Some mothers have shared frustration with their teens' cleaning methods. I remember one mother described her daughter as cleaning the same thing over and over instead of getting it done and moving on to the next thing. She repetitively wiped down the same kitchen cupboard without moving to the next, or she spent too long cleaning a small bathroom. I remember my daughter constantly apologized for having not cleaned my own bathroom shower very well. I never understood what she meant until I realized she was frustrated by not being able to more thoroughly clean the grout or caulking. When we talked about it, I found that she had not differentiated between cleaning something and trying to make it look brand new. I clarified for her what I wanted to see after a cleaning and the problem dissolved. Now I encourage parents to talk to their teens about what they expect to see after a cleaning, task, or chore.

Academics

Many parents grieve over their teens' academic status. As discussed previously, I have seen academics improve time and again regardless of age. Many teens start NDD therapy unable to read or write and yet within three years are finally reading and writing. Some advance more rapidly than others, but I have consistently seen progress when the teens and their parents stay the course. Some teens transfer out of a special education program into a 501 (mainstream classes with slight accommodations such as extended time on tests). Other teens no longer require any accommodations. Some begin to read and write; others progress faster than ever before. Parents who fear it may be too late for their teen should never, ever give up!

Driving

I have observed in teens parallels between riding a bicycle and learning to drive during or following their NDD therapy. When my daughter finally mastered riding a bicycle, it was because we gave her a bike with the brakes on the pedals, and the seat was lowered so that her feet could rest comfortably on the ground. She started out stopping with her feet and gradually adjusted to using the brakes. Once she mastered control of the bicycle and balance was in place, she was ready to start watching traffic, crossing streets, and maneuvering around pedestrians. The same thing occurred when learning to drive. At first she was terrified of the controls in the car. As soon as she saw another moving vehicle in a parking lot, her hands instantly came off the wheel and she stopped the car. In time, she adjusted and sensed her ability to control the car, and then she was able to focus more on traffic, turns, lane changes, etc. We all learn to drive through the same process. It takes a bit longer for some than for others.

A few parents have shared that their new-at-driving

teens seem slow at judging distance for turns, they back out of the driveway awkwardly, or they struggle with driving a car into a garage. These are normal problems with learning to drive. We learn some parts of driving more easily than others, and some things require more practice for certain individuals. In my experience, every teen who is developmentally ready to drive has eventually mastered it. My daughter was well into her 20s before she obtained her driver's license, but she did what I at one time thought would never happen. One day she decided she was ready. She called a driving school, paid for her classes, and passed the test on her first attempt.

We cannot rush teens into growing up, especially when they are in the midst of neuro-developmental delay therapy. When I finally decided I would humbly walk beside my daughter instead of pushing her toward age-appropriate behavior, I found wonderful things each step of the way. I learned that it was better for her if I slowed down and allowed her to progress at her own pace. I

> We cannot rush teens into growing up, especially when they are in the midst of neuro-developmental delay therapy.

watched as she recaptured phases of childhood and teen years and experienced for the first time many things she had missed along the way.

The process of NDD therapy is truly a journey. It is not easy, nor is it fast. As a parent who has been through it with a teen, I can wholeheartedly say, it was absolutely worth it.

Chapter 14

Parents and NDD Therapy: How to Help Your Child

Parents often ask how they can most help their children during their children's NDD therapy program. First, I emphasize the necessity of consistency with the assigned exercise. The key to success is consistency on a daily basis. In my experience, families who have not made the exercise a daily habit end up doing it on a hit-and-miss basis, and progress slows down tremendously.

> The key to success is consistency on a daily basis.

Exercise Time

I encourage parents to handle the exercise time at home in a relaxed manner, especially when their child's exercise targets the Moro Reflex. If parents approach those few minutes as if they have all the time in the world, they create an atmosphere that allows the child to relax. If a parent is hurried and rushed, the child is not as easily able to relax and allow the exercise to appropriately do what it needs to do. The more relaxed the environment, the better the experience for the child.

Journaling

Parents who journal the process benefit tremendously. Most parents hit emotional highs and lows during the therapy program. Between office visits, they will sometimes become discouraged or feel as though nothing has changed, nothing is different. Those who journal have shared that when those moments come, they review journal notes and are encouraged once again. A two-fold benefit, parents' journaling also helps me as a therapist. Parents who come to office visits with their journal notes have significantly more to share than those who do not. This enables me to better follow and understand how their children are responding to the therapy and to the changes.

Here are a mother's comments about journaling the experience:

I don't know about you, but I can barely remember what happened the last couple of weeks or even days depending on how crazy life gets. What I began doing is journaling about our day. The good, the bad and the ugly. Yes, even my ugly moments. I try to do this each evening. I know that seems tough, but what I have found is that when I look back in my mind at weeks or days past, it all runs together as the flow of life. When I journal, whether it be daily or every couple of days, I am more aware of things to notice and pay attention to. I have also found that it is so helpful for Anna, because it gives her a glimpse at all the things that have really occurred over the past weeks. She notices things I didn't even pay attention to. We both discover things that neither of us would have known if I came in and just tried spewing the past weeks to her. I know that it is difficult to see progress and change without doing this. We had a time frame that was just a blur to me. Somehow I did journal during this time. When we went in to see Anna and she asked how things were going, all I could share with her were the poor behavior/attitude I had seen in the last week. When we sat down and went through the journal, it was so opposite of my emotionally based answer. There were gold nuggets of progression everywhere!!! I was so thankful that I had taken the time to journal! It did not allow me to stay in that place of being completely discouraged and wondering if therapy was working. My son and our family are growing and changing so quickly! Journaling has also allowed me to see where my son is growing and trying to mature and where we as a family may be holding on to past attitudes or responses that may need shifting and altering on our parts. He cannot grow and change if we don't do it with him. I have found journaling to be such an important part of therapy that I hope to never go without it.

Discipline

Parents are encouraged to expect their children to demonstrate behaviors commonly associated with much younger children. Many parents have shared that they find themselves repeatedly saying things like, "Act your age." Most of these children are unable to do that, at least in given situations. I encourage parents to instead ask themselves what age their child is manifesting at any given moment, and then respond as if their child is the age of the demonstrated behavior. As maturity of the central nervous system comes, behavior gradually becomes more age appropriate.

For children who have intense emotions and anger, I suggest that parents not change their mode of discipline, and instead think about their child's emotional state. When a child with a strong Moro Reflex is exploding with rage or weeping uncontrollably, or whatever behavior is rapidly escalating to the point of losing control, the best thing a parent can do is remain calm and in control. Yelling, harsh words, high-pitched voices, and escalation of a parent's emotions are not what the child needs. Many children are aware of their own lack of self-control. During a moment of intense emotions, they need assurance that their parent will remain in control for both of them. In the child's mind, if parent and child both lose control, all is lost and fear reigns. A parent who remains in control provides relief and refuge for an overly emotional child. Once I realized this with my own daughter, the dynamics of our relationship and our home life changed. She stopped escalating! As anger and emotions surfaced in her behavior or attitude, I consciously made the decision to not escalate or show my exasperation. Instead, I forced myself to remain calm, reminded her of the consequences of her act or decision, and held my ground without lifting my voice or demonstrating anger or frustration. She often started to escalate but when I did not follow, her emotions plateaued or diminished. Over time, she began to show self-control. As the primitive reflexes withdrew, she no longer lost control and then gradually learned appropriate ways to deal with anger and frustration.

> A parent who remains in control provides relief and refuge for an overly emotional child.

I see this same fearful pattern in other children. In most cases, the children gradually become aware of their inappropriate or explosive behavior and express a desire to change. The awareness has to come first. Then we can talk about ways in which to learn and practice self-control. Before the awareness comes, and while the primitive reflexes dominate, children cannot reason out their behaviors — behaviors are involuntary and reflexive, just like a hammer to the knee.

Children who once were seemingly unable to be disciplined, corrected or given consequences change, and parents who change with them see great gains. I remember a 13-year-old girl who when I first met her came into my office as though in another world. She did not make eye contact, paced the room, talked to herself, and played with the window blinds. She did not acknowledge me at all, even when I asked her to leave the blinds alone. This happened during nearly every visit until about a year into her NDD therapy. During that year, she had begun making eye contact, showed less pacing, and started answering questions. One day, as she started to play with the blinds, I asked her to please leave them alone. She said, "Okay," and walked away. I knew then that she was ready to process and understand correction and consequences.

> Children who once were seemingly unable to be disciplined, corrected or given consequences change, and parents who change with them see great gains.

Another mother struggled with her son's lack of response when she called him, corrected him, or needed his immediate attention. She repeated herself endlessly. The boy's teacher reported the same thing. Unless his teacher tapped him on the shoulder, she experienced great difficulty with gaining his attention. As this boy neared completion of NDD therapy, and after the listening therapy, I witnessed the same behavior. He ignored both his mother and me. We found ourselves repeating things again and again. I thought this was out of place and that he should have had the ability to hear and respond. When I gained his attention, I asked him what it was I had said to him when he first came into the office. He repeated what I had said almost verbatim! He admitted that he was fully aware of what others have said, asked, or required of him, but that he did not want to listen or stop what he preferred to be doing. The issue had become his decision to ignore others and not an inability to pay attention. His mother left the office with ideas and plans for implementing consequences each time her son chose to ignore either of his parents and planned to talk with his teacher about classroom consequences as well.

Screen Time

Parents often tremendously help their children by turning off the TV and cutting back or eliminating "screen time": DS, iPad, iPod, cell phone games, computer, and video and Wii games. I have seen, more often than not, that children are typically overstimulated by screen time. I know many children who started sleeping better when screen time was eliminated, especially during the evening hours.

I remember starting therapy with a ten-year-old boy whose mother agreed to completely turn off the TV, and he did not have access to any other screens. I saw him again eight weeks later. The changes were astounding. The boy calmly sat in my office, made eye contact, and engaged in conversation. Eight weeks prior, he was hyper, constantly moving about, tuned out to anything I said — behavioral symptoms of overstimulation.

I truly think if I were to point an imaginary remote control at an overstimulated child and say, "Pause!" the child would stop instantly and I would have his or her immediate attention. Many children mimic the rapid activity they see on screens. It is as if they become what they just viewed on a screen. Too many children are becoming obsessed with technology and screen games. I believe when we allow this to happen without curfews we are teaching children to engross themselves into virtual reality and anti-social behavior. Ironically, these same things are considered symptomatic of autism or the autistic spectrum. I see a culture that is allowing children to shift into behavioral and learning disabilities because we adults cannot seem to tell them "no" and turn off the electronics.

I have visited classrooms in which teachers have asked specific children whose behavior was extreme (either "bouncing off the walls" or nearly comatose) if they had been watching TV prior to coming to school that day. These teachers said they consistently observe obvious differences in some children's day-to-day behaviors depending *...children are being taught to ignore sounds.* on whether or not those children watch TV prior to going to school.

Other teachers describe students who show extremely poor attention and seem to ignore instructions or directions, as if oblivious to being verbally addressed. During parent-teacher conferences, these teachers often learn that at home the TV is nearly always turned on, whether or not anyone is watching. In these environments, children are being taught to ignore sounds. The daily practice is to continually tune out sounds. And then adults wonder why their children tune them out.

Homeschool Advantage

Parents who homeschool their children have the advantage, particularly when it comes to helping a child with neuro-developmental delay, because they have flexibility that schools cannot provide. The length of the school day may need to be shortened or broken up for a time; the child may be at one grade level in one subject and at a vastly different grade level in another subject, which can be accommodated. Reading, writing, and math can be conducted according to the child's developmental age. The "classroom" environment can be organized according to the child's immediate needs, which can also be modified as the child increases in maturity.

Another advantage to homeschooling is the ability to individualize. Not only can parents provide flexibility in their teaching and "classroom," but they can also easily recognize the point at which their children have maximized their potential at any given moment in any subject. I remember as a homeschooling mother I could easily recognize when one of my children's eyes glazed over, showing we had just hit a moment of "I don't get it." This enabled me to immediately identify the stopping point, either for the day or for that moment. Maybe later, or on another day we could pick up where we left off. Such "moments" may be due to the time of day, fatigue, difficult subject material, or illness — any number of reasons. The parent, however, is able to instantly respond.

Homeschooled children are not as subject to bullying, which too often comes from peers in a classroom, and even occasionally from school professionals. I have heard parents tell about having been bullied by school staff regarding their children's behaviors or academic needs. I myself have been harassed and bullied by a few school specialists. I have witnessed several cases in which children were diagnosed with autism or autistic spectrum disorder and never challenged academically through their special education programs. Once the children's behavior settled down through NDD therapy, the schools did not pick up the pace academically until the parents protested. Even then, the children progressed at a faster rate from work the parents provided outside of the school system. On the other hand, several teachers and specialists have called and asked what they could do to facilitate a given child's NDD therapy. In the last few years, I have met some wonderful teachers who search for ways in which to help children in their classrooms. Special education teachers and school principals have increasingly shown curiosity and support for children's NDD therapy programs.

As the primitive reflexes withdraw, children's emotions should calm down and behavior should become more within a "normal" range. Sensory irregularities should significantly reduce, and children should overall seem more content inside their bodies and more comfortable with the world around them. Personalities typically emerge more strongly and parents become fully acquainted with who their children are — their interests, what motivates and energizes them, their full potential. I gradually became acquainted with my daughter as we both "rode the waves" of NDD therapy. I am thrilled to finally know who she is and what makes her tick. I enjoy hearing her thoughts and ideas, whether or not I agree. She is no longer dependent — what I for too long feared would be her destiny. While parents may not like absolutely everything they see in their children, they do want to see them as complete and whole individuals. We parents want to see our children grow from infanthood, through childhood, past the teens, and into adulthood. NDD therapy is doing that for hundreds of children.

Chapter 15

A Complex Organism: Regarding Diets, Supplements, and Wellness

Children who experience neuro-developmental delay may very likely struggle with food absorption, adrenal function, circulation, immunity, or overall wellness. I see this, in some cases, as perhaps a result of developmental delay. Because the human body is a complex organism, what is experienced in one area will naturally affect other areas as well. For example, if I cut my finger and it bleeds, my finger is not the only part of me that is affected. The immune system begins a detection process and sends white blood cells to the scene. Blood vessels constrict in order to staunch the bleeding. The skin responds, perhaps with inflammation, and starts the healing process. I might agonize mentally about how much my finger hurts and think of nothing else for a time. Prescription medications list potential side effects for that very reason — a medicine prescribed for one ailment may affect other areas in the body as well. Likewise, if the central nervous system shows delay in development, other systems and organs in the body may just as likely be delayed in development. I have seen enough children become physically and physiologically stronger during NDD therapy (nothing else was changed or added regarding diet or supplements during that time) to believe that stimulation toward maturity of the brain stem may affect more than one area of functionality in a given individual.

If a child I meet for the first time is following a specific protocol from a health professional, I do not suggest any deviations. Many times, a health professional has monitored changes during the time in which a child participates in NDD therapy and altered the child's protocol as needed. A sign of change! I remember a girl I worked with who up through age eight underwent annual colonoscopies because of recurring polyps. After NDD therapy, her physician ceased the annual exams because polyps were no longer found. Other children, after years of suffering with asthma or allergies, have shown incredible changes for the better. I have known children who required frequent use of inhalers, and during or after NDD therapy, inhalers were no longer needed.

If a child has not followed a particular diet or protocol by the time we meet, I am slow to discuss any possible changes regarding diet or supplements. Stimulation at the brain stem level may affect the vagus nerve, the vestibular system, and the autonomic nervous system so that maturity of the central nervous system in its entirety might come about naturally.

To Diet or Not to Diet

In ten years of practice as a neuro-developmental delay therapist, I have found that often, though not always, dietary factors play a role in a child's progress through NDD therapy. Many children, when I first meet them, have already been following strict or special diets. For some, the diets make all the difference for their nutritional and health needs. For others, strict adherence to a particular diet over long periods of time effects no change. Every person is different; there is no "magic cure" that will work in every situation or with every child. Instead, a more holistic approach, one that looks at development from before birth and considers the roles of the digestive and immune systems, allows one to see the overall functioning — or lack of functioning — in any given child.

My daughter, at age 18, was reduced to six foods. In her case, we finally learned that she had toxic levels of zinc in her gut. After using Chinese herbs for about four months, she felt and acted completely differently. The changes in her behavior and her own description of how she sensed the improvement in digestion indicated significant change. Gradually, we introduced new foods into her diet over the next year until she was able to eat whatever she chose, within reason.

I have observed some interesting situations in which specific dietary modifications were necessary and positive changes resulted. This is the key: the effects of the diet should be observable and beneficial. I remember working with one seven-year-old girl who refused to eat the foods listed in her specific diet protocol. I told her mother that if she were my child and throwing her food instead of eating it, I would feed her, for now, what she will eat. The mother decided to do just that, and as the girl advanced through NDD therapy, she gradually initiated a desire to try new foods. She stopped losing weight and her diet expanded without negative results.

> This is the key: the effects of the diet should be observable and beneficial.

Eating and Developmental Delay

Several children refused to chew foods when I first met them. They desired drinks and easy-to-swallow foods only. These children's aversion to chewing matched the phase of development I observed during the NDD assessment — in every single case, the child showed minimally- or fully-retained Moro and Rooting reflexes. Some of these children spent a period of time eating pureed or baby food until a desire to chew surfaced. As the children showed increased withdrawal of the Moro and Rooting reflexes, they began to feed themselves chewable foods.

For some children, better eating habits are all that is needed. Whole, real foods, instead of processed foods, might make a significant difference. Some children digest meals better when proteins and starches are separated. Vegetables with either a protein or a starch are more easily digested. A hamburger without the bun and with vegetables is easier to digest than a hamburger with a bun and French fries.

Foods can Alter Behavior

Milk and other dairy products affect behavior in some children just as much as sugar, refined foods, food dyes, or food allergies affect others. I remember a girl who was always as sweet as could be when I visited with her. One day her mother showed me a video on her cell phone of the girl having a temper tantrum. In the video, she screamed, ranted and raved, gritted her teeth, and once she realized she was being video-taped, flew into an unbelievable rage. She was not destructive, just out of control emotionally. I suggested that her mother remove dairy from her diet for three months and observe. Dairy was her problem. As long as this girl stays away from dairy, she is a delight. I have routinely found a connection between dairy intake and raging or violent behavior. Food dyes have been a source of raging behavior in a few children.

Some mothers have found that their children can tolerate a little bit of sugar if they eat it after a meal and not on an empty stomach. Behavior becomes intolerable when they eat sweets or processed foods on empty stomachs. I have found that sugar may contribute to hyperactivity and even insomnia in some children.

Several mothers and I have suspected their children had parasites. When these mothers supplemented their children's diets with herbal remedies to eliminate parasites, behavior became less hyperactive, the children were better able to focus and stay on task, and bowel movements became regulated.

I remember a boy who struggled with peculiar behavior from the time his parents adopted him. I met him when he was four years old. By the time he was five, his parents and I talked about the possibility of him having parasites. They took the boy for specific tests, and several types of parasites were detected. He was given a specific protocol to follow for the next several months, and his behavior calmed down within a few days of starting the program.

Constipation

Numerous children suffer with constipation. Interestingly, many parents are unaware that this is an issue for their children. While some children may complain they hurt or cannot eliminate when they need to, others are oblivious to the problem. Constipation can affect moods and behavior and can cause headaches. Only when parents and I talk about it, and sometimes with the children, do we realize how serious the problem is. Constipation may be symptomatic of dehydration, lack of good digestion, or problems with elimination. Some children are unaware of the need to eliminate their bowels. Many children have a fear of using the toilets at their schools and resist the natural urge to defecate while at school.

Allergies

Allergies often must be considered during the process of NDD therapy. Allergies are generally an indicator of problems within the digestive system, and the vagus nerve is interrelated with digestion. The vagus nerve, which begins in the brain stem and goes to every major organ in the body, is actively involved in organ functions. Therefore, digestion may be affected by neuro-developmental delay beginning at the brain stem. As changes take place within the brain stem, the vagus nerve is stimulated and digestion may be affected in a positive manner. Two siblings I worked with were both highly allergic to various foods, especially certain food dyes. Both children took daily medication specifically for their allergies. Their allergies showed some improvement as they continued with NDD therapy without any changes to their medication. One day their mother called to say she had just finished reading the ingredients label on the medication bottle. The food dyes both children were allergic to were in the medication! She immediately stopped the medicine and in a short time all of their allergies completely disappeared. I believe their allergies disappeared due to better digestion and therefore they no longer required medication.

Yeast

Yeast is another problem for many children. Brain fog, slow thinking, and drowsiness are common symptoms; or hyperactivity and the inability to stay focused may be problematic. Observable symptoms of possible yeast overgrowth include thrush, athlete's foot, yeast infections, and cravings for sugar or carbs. I often suggest to parents of sugar-craving children that they supplement the diet with acidophilus for a bit and watch for a decrease in the cravings before they fight with their children about eliminating high-sugar foods. Teens have often been more willing to decrease their daily soda intake after a period of acidophilus supplements and subtle meal changes (such as less sugar and no sweet desserts other than fruit).

Homeopathy

Classical homeopathy has proven beneficial for many children with neuro-developmental delay. Homeopathic remedies use natural sources to stimulate the central nervous system into balancing itself. For children who have already shown an immaturity in the development of the central nervous system, homeopathy often dovetails nicely with NDD therapy, in my experience. Again, not all children are the same and not every child experiences NDD therapy in the same manner, so homeopathy is applicable when the need is apparent. I think of an adopted girl who progressed beautifully through NDD and the listening therapies, yet still struggled socially at school. Academics were good, she was active physically, but socially she still seemed withdrawn. She took one dose of a homeopathic remedy and her teacher and family were delighted. She developed many friendships, and her parents, months later, said they loved her interaction with guests in their home.

A teenager diagnosed with autism showed extreme behaviors. His father told me he would be content if his son could just reach the point in which his behavior was the same without meds as they observed currently with meds. Two years later, after NDD and listening therapies, as well as use of homeopathic remedies, their son was completely weaned off medications without adverse behavior.

High anxiety, extreme fears or sensitivities, hyperactivity, and other possible symptoms sometimes indicate the need for homeopathic remedies. Just as the needed remedy varies per person, the number of doses and length of time required between doses varies. I remember a boy who completed NDD and the listening therapies yet still showed extreme anger and impatience. After taking a specific remedy, his anger subsided and excellence in school accelerated.

NDD Therapy, Digestion and Overall Wellness

I have worked with a vast number of children who completed NDD therapy without their parents and me once discussing their diets or overall wellness. Some are on special protocols when I first meet them and others later show a need for something to change in their diets.

Once we have given NDD therapy time to do what it needs to do, we can better determine other needs — a process that can take several months. Maturity of the central nervous system through NDD therapy has shown improved digestion in some children. I have heard about decreases in allergy symptoms, reduction in the number of allergies, disappearances of allergies, better eating habits, regular elimination, improvement in or disappearance of asthma, and improved health overall. I can think of many children who came to visit me after at least a two-month gap and I hardly recognized them because they had suddenly grown taller and gained substantial weight. Instead of the weak, emaciated look with dark circles or bags under their eyes, they were full of life, filled out, and their eyes sparkled. They glowed with health and vitality, yet nothing had changed in their diets.

Parents are encouraged to not jump into changes right away or all at one time. While going through this process, parents have shared that for the first time they have seen something work for the better, without adverse side effects, and they commit to staying the course regardless of how long it may take. They repeatedly tell me that things are much better compared to the previous year. This is exactly how I felt as a parent. For the first time, when my daughter was nearly 19, progress was observable and changes were advancing. NDD and the listening therapies brought about tremendous maturity. Follow up dietary adjustments brought additional changes. I did not care how long it took; I was in it for the long haul. Nothing we had previously tried stimulated these deep, life-changing stages of growth. It was one baby-step after another, and well worth the effort.

PART 4:
JOURNEYS OF HOPE

Chapter 16

Doug

Doug, a young man who will soon graduate from high school, was 10 years old and in fourth grade when I first met him. During his almost two years of NDD therapy, I watched him progress from being angry, insecure, and unable to cope, to full of life, happy, confident, and socially and academically successful.

Doug's mother shared that his birth had been stressful; he suffered from low oxygen levels and was blue at birth. He required intensive care for a time. As a toddler, he suffered from recurring cysts in his inner ear. He disliked having his hair and nails cut. Doug never crawled on his hands and knees. Although his vocabulary had developed to advanced levels, expressive language lagged. By the time he started school, he was already struggling socially and academically.

His mother, a teacher, well understood the difficulties her son faced at school. He qualified for special education and was also labeled as having social and emotional difficulties. By the time he entered fourth grade, his mother described him as in "crisis." He was not functioning or thriving. His behavior was loud, overly dramatic and overreactive; he had a negative attitude and, at times, was overly apologetic. His mother said he complained about not having friends, but he had no motivation to try to make friends. He was judgmental toward others, and when he did attempt a few friendships, they did not work out due to incompatibility.

Several years later, he shared with me that he had known his peers were maturing faster than he was, and that had added to his anxiety.

At school, Doug was stressed and overwhelmed. He later said he had known that he exaggerated his struggles, could not organize himself or his work, could not keep up with the classroom environment, and he had been unable to cope with it or change it. Teachers reported that he often lay down on the floor away from others in his group, curled into a fetal position and went to sleep. He was on an individualized special-education program (IEP), and even then, the stress of school overwhelmed him. Life itself overwhelmed him. His parents did everything for him. Everyone in the family was drained, and his parents knew that Doug was aware of their frustration. They had tried several therapies and interventions, as well as specialized diets, yet nothing helped.

The parent of another child I worked with referred Doug's parents to me. His mother was excited at the prospect of pursuing this approach, but initially his father seriously questioned and doubted. Doug's father, at that time, worked closely with a well-known psychiatrist in the Denver area. I remember his first phone conversation with me, in which he challenged my knowledge and experience. Even so, a month after his initial assessment, Doug started NDD therapy.

I remember Doug as a negative, unhappy boy who doubted that anything would help him feel better about himself. He liked ridiculing politicians; I thought his dry sense of humor, for a boy his age, was paradoxically adult level. I remember feeling emotionally drained after our first meeting. I was distressed by the sadness and bitterness in such a young person.

Doug's first several months of NDD therapy were rocky. His family was committed to the program although Doug was angry and protested that this therapy would do nothing, just like those he had previously tried. When he came to see me for checkups, cursing was part of his regular vocabulary. He often told his mother in front of me that this was a waste of everyone's time and that I was just taking their money. I was so concerned about this boy's outlook on life that nothing he said offended me; instead, I was moved to diligently pray for him.

By the time Doug started fifth grade, remarkable changes had taken place. His mother said he was appropriately sleeping less, eating better, and getting more work done at school. He was also better organized, less stressed, and less overly dramatic. His voice was not as loud, and he was not "getting into people's faces." Doug was beginning to mature. I noted gradual, measured changes during this time related to the primitive reflexes, the vestibular system, and eye movements. I remember one day in particular, in which I knew for certain that Doug had turned a corner, and his life would never again be the same. He walked into my office, looked me in the eye, and his whole face lit up. His eyes sparkled and smiled. I was moved to the very core of my being. For the first time since I had met him, Doug looked truly happy and content with himself. I remember thinking he had become comfortable with life instead of overwhelmed by it. Life had dramatically changed for this boy, and I had been privileged to witness the change. I was also thrilled that Doug and I had become friends.

During Doug's sixth-grade year, his mother said he was taking care of himself and showing responsibility with his homework. He completed a year-long project for school and assumed complete responsibility in a timely manner. He surprised his teachers and parents with an impressive oral classroom presentation, a 20-minute speech about the United Nations in front of 90 students and parents. Each time his mother remembers that day, she continually says, "Unbelievable!" She said his self-esteem had begun to blossom in other ways as well. Friends began to gravitate toward Doug, and this time he was open and available with less stress and anxiety. During this year of school, Doug no longer required an IEP. His father became one of my strongest supporters and has since referred many families.

I remember one day Doug and his mother came into my office, and he asked me to follow him outside. He dragged his bicycle out of the back of his car, hopped on, and rode around the parking lot. He was proud to show me that he could now ride his bike with no hands.

I spoke with Doug and his mother about a year after he completed NDD therapy. Now a middle-school student, Doug said the pace of the therapy had been just right for him. He said it had been slow, challenging, and helpful. His mother said it had seemed slow during the whole process, but looking back at all the changes that had taken place, in hindsight, it happened quickly. Every time I think about Doug and his 18-month period of tremendous growth, my emotions are deeply stirred. Recently, his mother shared that now, at age 16, he works at a store helping out in all areas, while still a full-time high-school student. His boss prefers that Doug work the cash registers because he has strong social skills. What a change from a few years ago! I will continue to enjoy hearing about Doug's pursuits into adulthood, happy that I do so now as an outside observer. He is a confident, happy, and thriving young man.

Chapter 17

Josiah

Josiah reminds me of what we used to think of as the all-American boy. He, now 13, has blue eyes and a lot of freckles. He is filled out nicely, not skinny and not overweight, has short, closely-cut hair, and likes to wear plaid shirts with blue jeans. He is refreshingly innocent, which brings a smile to my face every time I think about him.

During her pregnancy with Josiah, his mother was told that the amniotic fluid was low, and the baby might have Down syndrome. He was born six-to-seven weeks early with the cord wrapped twice around his neck. He spent two days in intensive care because his lungs were not fully developed. Josiah did not have Down syndrome, but he definitely showed developmental delay from early on. He was hypersensitive to having his hair and nails cut. Cold sores frequently developed around his mouth, presumably from a habit of constantly licking his lips. He was a teeth grinder and often sucked on his shirts. Eye contact was poor. His head often shook side to side as if twitching. Speech and language development were delayed. He was unable to follow verbal instructions and equally struggled with verbal expression. He often repeated his mother verbatim. Separation anxiety was overwhelming when he was left with his grandmother as well as when he started kindergarten at the nearby public school. Relatives suggested perhaps Josiah was autistic.

Overall, Josiah was a shy, quiet boy. On his first day of kindergarten at public school, the principal called his mother to share his concerns about Josiah being an atypical student. Thereafter, the school observed him more closely and started pulling him out of class for assistance with his special needs. At a meeting with the school's special education director, occupational therapist, and principal, Josiah's mother was heartbroken as she watched them ask Josiah the color of the truck he held. He did not answer. They asked him the color of his shirt. He still did not answer. Josiah's mother thought, "I know where this is going." She did not want to pursue the route of having Josiah labeled and "stuck." A few months later, Josiah's parents pulled him out of the school, "never to return," and began homeschooling him as well as his older sister, a gifted student.

I first met Josiah when he was eight and technically a second grader. His mother had struggled with trying to teach him at home, as methods and curricula did not help. Several homeschooling mothers in a local support group referred her to me. She eventually inquired, having learned that I would not diagnose her son with a label and then teach the family how to cope with it.

In my first meeting with Josiah, he did not answer any questions I asked, and his mother tried to intervene. She repeated my questions, and Josiah repeated the questions back to her. She then gave him the answers to my questions, and he repeated the sentences word for word. For example, she said, "Tell Anna you ate a sandwich for lunch," and he repeated, "Tell Anna you ate a sandwich for lunch." I noticed occasional eye contact but never for longer than a few seconds. An initial assessment showed signs of neuro-developmental delay and auditory processing difficulties. Josiah struggled with following verbal directions; it was much easier for him to imitate my body positions than to carry out my instructions. Balance was difficult, and body awareness was poor. He gave the appearance of being lost inside his own body. Josiah showed retention of many of the primitive reflexes, vestibular dysfunction, and a lack of emergence of the postural reflexes. This boy was, in many ways, developmentally functioning at the brain stem level — what one would expect to see in a child up through age one.

Josiah started NDD therapy within three weeks of the assessment. I encouraged his mother to not push academics, because developmentally he was not ready. She presented subjects simply, and if Josiah showed frustration or complete lack of understanding, she let it go for the time being.

Within the first six to seven months, Josiah showed improved eye contact and stopped grinding his teeth. He started coloring inside the lines, sketching creative drawings of his own, and completing puzzles and mazes. He was still a picky eater and emotionally frustrated, but he also began active play. During this time, he began to look as though he fit inside his body better. He stopped repeating what was said to him. One day I asked him, "What did you have for lunch today?" He gazed around the room for a few seconds and then said, "My…My dad has a truck." I was excited! Though he had not answered my question, he had communicated with me for the first time.

Nearing the end of his first year of NDD therapy,

Josiah showed some inhibition of the primitive reflexes and improved balance and vestibular function. Eye movements had improved tremendously. These changes manifested in obvious ways to those in Josiah's life. He had begun to sit still when a family member read him a story. The fidgetiness was gone. His mother said he had become a good eater, stopped licking his lips unless the weather was extremely dry, and was able to stay overnight at his grandmother's. One day when he came to see me, I asked as usual, "What did you have for lunch today?" He looked right at me and said, "I had a hamburger." I nearly cried.

A year into his program, Josiah, age nine, completed the 60-hour sound therapy program. Afterward, his mother attended a writing workshop our office offered and began teaching him basic writing. His letters were large and unevenly spaced, and he needed a lot of coaching in order to write a simple, complete sentence. But new things continued to emerge. Josiah was now able to follow simple verbal directions, and he was beginning to read. Bedwetting stopped. His mother said he now enjoyed having his hair cut. Josiah's sister said she no longer felt embarrassed or frustrated by his behavior around others. His parents shared that they felt like their family life was becoming normal. Josiah began singing and remembering words to songs. He recited Bible verses. Verbal expression was maturing — now when he spoke four-to-five-word sentences, they made sense. Within a short period of time, he started verbalizing more complex sentences. He began conversing with adults, and his social skills improved. He also started asking questions about the world around him. Analytical thought processes were emerging.

Relatives and neighbors inquired about the obvious, delightful changes in Josiah. His maternal grandmother shared that she noticed tremendous improvements regarding verbal expression and the ability to converse and interact with his cousins. For the first time, he began to demonstrate a desire for closer relationships with his extended family. He also began showing independence. On his own initiative, he started writing letters to his paternal grandparents. After writing each letter, he sealed it in an envelope, found the address in his mother's book, and addressed the envelope — all on his own. Josiah's parents began receiving continual "kudos" from relatives, including comments such as, "Whatever you're doing for Josiah is absolutely wonderful!" Various relatives said they now observed him engaging with others instead of being withdrawn, socially "outside," and awkward. He had become confident; he was no longer easily upset but was calmer and less anxious. His family described him as better able to manage and control his emotions. Extended family members were pleased and surprised to hear Josiah answer their phone calls and then be able to converse over the phone. Neighbors noticed the changes as well. Josiah was blossoming.

Josiah continued NDD therapy a second year and made tremendous strides academically, socially, and emotionally. Almost exactly one year after the listening therapy, he started a 20-hour sound therapy boost, and new things began to surface. His mother said she could see more of his personality emerging as well as growth in overall maturity. He started demonstrating responsibility with chores and completing some of his schoolwork independently. He began playing games and wanted to try new ones. He became more outgoing and wanted to do things on his own, such as buy a soda at the store and pay for it by himself with his own money. He also started arguing a bit now and then with his sister, demonstrating typical sibling confrontations. He often came into our office ahead of his mother and asked, "How are you today?" or shared a story or event. This was a long way from "Tell Anna what you had for lunch"! He was no longer a quiet, withdrawn, disconnected boy.

Josiah showed more retention in day-to-day learning, and reading and writing showed continued growth. He began reading sentences and beginner books although comprehension was extremely weak. I encouraged his parents to listen to him read aloud for about 15 minutes daily and to interrupt after phrases or very short sentences to ask comprehension questions. At this point, however, he was not able to comprehend a complete paragraph after reading it aloud. He started writing complete sentences with help, which developed into writing short paragraphs with help.

As part of his homeschooling, Josiah and I met for one-on-one tutoring one hour each week. This was truly a joy for me because, through our time together, I was able to consistently observe new things in his development. Handwriting improved nicely so that letter and word spacing were no longer awkward. Reading comprehension slowly improved. He began understanding and telling jokes. He shared stories about family vacations and his dog, and he asked questions about my family. We have shared good conversations. I cherish these, because not so long ago, this was nonexistent. Math remained difficult and sometimes grasping new concepts was slow. But growth was steady.

When I had first met Josiah, he showed no facial expressions; then, one day, I noticed his face was full of expression. I wondered how long it had been since this had changed and I had simply taken it for granted and not noticed it. He smiled broadly or showed excitement with raised eyebrows. Expressions matched emotions, and body language was evident.

Three years and five months after I met Josiah, I retested him once more regarding NDD. The primitive reflexes had inhibited, and postural reflexes were emerging. His vestibular system showed improvement with slight dysfunction, so I suggested exercises that target the vestibular system at the brain stem level.

A month later, new and obvious changes occurred. He completed a 52-step Lego fire station project by himself by following the pictorial directions. He started writing notes on a whiteboard while watching history videos for school. I suggested that his mother start trying new things in math, such as learning to tell time on an analog clock. Only a month later, Josiah was able to tell time by the minute and understand beginning concepts of time, such as, "It takes 20 minutes to do such-and-such."

I also suggested that he should start learning to count money with only dimes and pennies at first, because their values are consistent with simple addition — 10s and ones. Within a short time, he was counting money not only with dimes and pennies but also quarters and nickels. He also began adding numbers without the use of manipulatives and showed a new understanding of basic concepts in multiplication. One day, on his own initiative, he wrote and solved several double-digit addition problems — a first!

Writing noticeably improved. During my weekly sessions with Josiah, I found that he was able to keep his thoughts together so that when he wrote a paragraph the sentences flowed from one to the next without my assistance. He quickly moved into writing multi-paragraph papers. He started bringing me papers he wrote about various presidents of the U.S. and shared verbal stories about some of his favorites.

Josiah's reading showed notable improvement with inflection, including pauses at commas and periods. Reading comprehension also advanced dramatically. During one of our weekly sessions, I asked Josiah to read aloud from Roald Dahl's book *George's Marvelous Medicine*. His comprehension was excellent. I enjoyed listening to his own comments inserted periodically, like "Oh, gross!" when George's grandma talked about liking to eat worms, beetles, and earwigs. He was able to understand and explain unusual terms the author used in the story such as a reference to "grandma" as "the old girl." Josiah was also easily able to give me a character description of both George and his grandma.

I taught Josiah to spell based on sound. He gradually learned to self-edit and now does a remarkable job of it. Recently I dictated the word "instead." Josiah wrote it as "intead." I asked him to read what he wrote, and as he did, he immediately corrected his error. Self-correction has become consistent in all his writing. As a result, his spelling has been phenomenally good. I noticed that, for a long time, he spelled from my dictation without regard for vocabulary development. He never asked the meaning of a given word but simply wrote from dictation. At about the same time that math and reading significantly advanced, Josiah started asking for definitions of spelling words. Not only did he ask for meanings, but then he voluntarily used the words in sentences. He also showed increased thought processing. For example, one day I dictated the word "headlight." I asked Josiah if he knew what the word meant, and he explained it well. Then he asked, "What are the lights at the back of a car called?" On another occasion, I dictated the word "leather." Josiah wrote it and then asked, "Where does leather come from?" These are examples of thought processes that, for a long time, were nonexistent for Josiah.

When Josiah describes another person, his focus is more on character than physical attributes — a quality I admire and appreciate. For example, one day I asked him to tell me more about a neighbor he had mentioned. He described the man's kindness, concern for others, helpful attitude, and so forth. I knew more about the man's character than I knew about his physical appearance, yet it is much easier to describe a person physically.

This has been quite a journey for Josiah and his family. His family and I have been astonished and thrilled to tears with all that has changed in the last four years. His story was not an overnight miracle, but it has been a miracle nonetheless. I credit his parents for their commitment and diligence to provide what Josiah has needed and their unwillingness to accept a label and expect Josiah to cope with it for the rest of his life. Every time I think of Josiah or his family, I cannot help but smile and thank God for the privilege of being a part of their lives.

Chapter 18

Paul

Paul is an impressive young man. Always cheerful and optimistic, he seems to wear a perpetual smile. At age 17 his reading-aloud and writing skills were negligible; at age 24, he is married with two children and recently graduated from college with a degree in chemistry. Unbelievable!

My first encounter with Paul and his parents was at an introductory seminar where I presented NDD therapy. About a month later, when he was 17 ½ years old, they came to my office for an assessment. Afterward, his mother said Paul expressed a strong desire to pursue the therapy even though he had struggled through many previous interventions.

His mother described Paul as having dyslexic symptoms. In kindergarten, he refused any and all writing or drawing utensils and thought schoolwork was optional. He chose to opt out! When his kindergarten teacher finally persuaded him to pick up a crayon to draw his family, he grabbed a black crayon and viciously drew spiraling circles on his paper. The family knew by the time he was in first grade that something was amiss.

During his first week of first grade, the school called his parents to suggest a special education program. Mid-year, Paul's mother discovered that the words he "read" had all been memorized. He was unable to sound out even simple words. Thus began Paul's homeschooling years.

As Paul's mother tried to teach him, she became as frustrated as he already was. Every time she insisted he engage in any kind of school work, his whole body shook and tears ran down his face. She said he could not finish anything or follow the simplest of directions. He would complete his school work in their basement in order to avoid hearing normal house noises such as the ticking of a clock. He later shared with me that noises in the house had distracted him. His parents tried curriculum after curriculum, but nothing helped. Basic reading did not start for Paul until he was 12 years old. Language arts had pretty much been on the back burner. When he did write, he composed long run-on sentences. Paul informed me that he had never grasped the need or purpose for periods, commas, capital letters, and so forth.

I met Paul when he was 17 and thought he had a winning personality. He was cheerful, enthusiastic, able to laugh at himself, eager to please, and desperately wanted to achieve academically. When asked to read aloud from a beginner *I Can Read* book, he stumbled and often changed words. After he wrote a long, run-on sentence, I asked him to read it back to me because I was unable to decipher it. He could not read it either. He did not know and could not tell me even what he thought he had written.

The process of NDD therapy was hard for Paul and his family. During the first week, he struggled with periods of nausea and brain fog or "fuzziness" as he described it. His mother said his appetite decreased so that he ate less and sometimes skipped meals. He started sleeping through his alarm clock. But by the second week, the alarm clock was startling him awake.

Academically, Paul's mother thought he was regressing, showing less attention and less recall of previously learned material. Math showed some good days and some bad days. Overall, academics were inconsistent day-to-day. At about the same time, Paul's interest in physical activities waned. He had always liked to ride his bike, run, and lift weights, but he suddenly showed less motivation for physical activities.

During Paul's second month of NDD therapy, he became more "antsy" and fidgety. He struggled with getting to sleep, and sleep was more difficult. He either started dreaming or could finally remember his dreams. He described a desire to bang his head against a wall. His mother said he often crossed his arms over his chest, curled his shoulders and slammed himself into door jambs. When he did this in the car, she offered to pull over for fear he might break the passenger door window. When Paul was preoccupied or mentally engaged in something, he was antsy, but when he did not have something in particular on his mind, the desire to bang his head into a wall surfaced. His mother described this period of time as "definite regression."

Paul is an amazing pianist, having played since he was young, and his family observed that playing became a good way for him to release tension. His mother said he played "intensely beautiful" music during these times. New body movements appeared, such as jerky head movements and a thrusting of his arms, and eventually the desire to bang his head against the wall decreased. Toward the end of the month, Paul's desire for physical activity picked back up, but not yet to the level he had prior to starting the therapy. He regained his appetite as well. His mother said he was still "antsy, but of the less consistent variety."

Paul struggled with what should have been simple tasks. His mother said he had trouble following directions and carrying them out as well as he did prior to starting the therapy. Thought processes that required an understanding of cause and effect or sequential steps in routine activities became more difficult. His mother reported, "One night he was sitting on our big exercise ball in the dining room while we were sitting around talking. He lost his balance and fell backward, shattering the glass to the built-in china hutch."

Paul's struggles led him to sense regression from within. He started losing for the first time ever at a computer strategy game. He struggled with getting to sleep. What little he had been able to read was harder for him to comprehend. He said he felt confused. Piano playing deteriorated; he was klutzy and clumsy. But, on the other hand, he took apart a wireless mouse, and using Lego and Lego robotics, created a device that would turn on his computer music.

Well into his third month of NDD therapy, things began to improve. Sleeping came easier. He started responding to directions more calmly, showing better control of his emotions. Developmental maturity of the central nervous system was evident and measurable. Oculo-motor (eye movement) functions such as convergence, tracking, hand-eye tracking, and accommodation all showed tremendous improvement. During this same time, Paul took a math placement test at the local community college and scored solidly for starting classes at the algebra level. He signed up for a music theory class, algebra, and a martial arts class. I urged him to hold off on the algebra class for the time being, but he was anxious to show what he could do.

The listening therapy started during Paul's fourth month of NDD therapy, when he was 18 years old. Almost immediately his mother noticed a disruption with his auditory processing. He became more mentally scattered than usual when following auditory commands. His father thought he started reversing the number "5" more often. Paul began struggling with attention and general productivity. Periods of dizziness started, which frustrated him because he wanted to keep a busy schedule. The changes in his nervous system not only affected desires and energy, but also forced him to slow down. He realized he needed to change his status in the algebra class to audit, and he later withdrew from the class altogether. On the positive side, Paul one day shared with his mother that he was all of a sudden able to clearly hear and differentiate between sounds in the words "melody" and "medley." Although he had understood the definitions, both words had, up to this point, always sounded the same. Not only was this profound regarding auditory processing, it was also necessary and appreciated because music has always been a major part of his life.

During the break between the two halves of the listening therapy, Paul's mother said he still seemed scattered, poor at following instructions, and unable to remember where he placed things. "He lost the lock to the utility trailer hitch — and my keys with it (about $300.00 to replace it all)... he's now in that mode where if he misplaces something he hasn't a CLUE what might have happened to it."

The second half of the listening therapy started, and

Paul's mother said he began sleeping through his alarm again, or he would turn it off and go back to sleep. Jerky behavior increased again, as well as agitation. One day his mother told him he needed to write his birthday thank-you notes. He moaned, groaned, and paced the room as if in physical pain. In order to try to calm himself, he went outside and grabbed a Wiffle ball. When he threw it against the house, it broke a hole in the siding.

As I worked with Paul during his final six hours of the listening therapy, dramatic changes began. He was able, for the first time ever, to spell words sound-by-sound. No twitching, no anxiety. He then began to write sentences from dictation (by sound) without physical aggravation. Simultaneously, he was able to expand written sentences, create compound sentences, and maintain creativity in his writing — all while spelling by sound.

A year after starting NDD therapy, Paul and I met for tutoring sessions — one-hour sessions, four days each week, in reading, writing, and spelling — for the next eight months. He continued with classes at the local community college. During that time, I watched academics advance at a much faster rate than I ever would have guessed. The physical pain associated with academic work lessened and then disappeared. He slowly began to read some of his textbooks and received help with others. He started writing his own papers with help in final editing. He shared that his love of music was the same, but for the first time, he felt a meshing of abilities. He used to write poems and lyrics and musical scores but had never been able to combine them into songs. The ability to do just that emerged, and Paul began composing music well enough that a record company offered him a contract for a CD. After just over a year-and-half, Paul no longer needed my help. With the NDD barriers now gone, Paul's natural talents exploded. His progress amazed me profoundly. Many children I work with blossom with abilities as they complete NDD therapy, but Paul's progress was unbelievably rapid.

Paul stayed in touch, a delightful benefit for me. He shared interesting things when we occasionally visited. In his first college English class, his final grade was a B; in his second class, he received an A. His English professor shared that Paul's writing talent could lead to him becoming a novelist if he so chose.

I was elated beyond words when I opened my office door one afternoon and observed Paul sitting in a chair engrossed in a chemistry textbook. It was unbelievable how far he had come, and in such a short period of time!

Several years have passed. Paul is now married and has two children. As a husband and father, he continued his schooling while working full-time and recently completed a university degree in chemistry. He is also a trained EMT and personal trainer. I recently visited with his parents. His father said, "When we met you, he couldn't fill out a job application." His mother said, "[NDD therapy] was a hard process. Paul went from coping to dropping down into being a wreck and finally to coming out of it a better musician and better student." She said she had always known he was highly intelligent and was now thrilled to finally see him whole. The entire process was truly a journey of hope. They stuck it out and remained hopeful when doubts arose. The rough journey ended and a promising new future awaits.

End Notes

1   Buck, Anna. 2008. Miracle Children: Behavior and Learning Disabilities Uprooted. Broomfield, Colorado: Anna's House LLC, 43.

2   Ibid, 40-41.

3   Ibid, 42-43.

4   Ibid, 37-38.

5   Ibid, 44.

6   Ayres, A. Jean, PhD. 1979. Sensory Integration and the Child. Los Angeles, California: Western Psychological Services, 37.

7   Eliot, Lise. 2000. What's Going on in There?: New York, New York: Bantam Books, 149-150.

8   Ibid, 151.

About the Author

Anna Buck, author of *Miracle Children*, is the founder and director of Anna's House, LLC (2005).

Anna spent over 30 years in the educational field and pursued advanced studies in England (The Institute for Neuro-Physiological Psychology), Canada (The Listening Fitness Centre), and Scotland (Sheila Dobie Associates (Training) Ltd.). She is certified by ANCB as a Certified Traditional Naturopath and completed coursework at the New England School of Homeopathy. These trainings have allowed her to approach children's difficulties and disabilities from a developmental and holistic perspective.

Anna's House has worked with hundreds of children from all over the United States. Many come with behavioral and/or learning difficulties. An initial assessment determines the point of breakdown within the central nervous system and therapy begins at that point, most generally at the brain stem level. A child's specific program is based on retracing normal patterns of developmental growth that, for most children, begins at stages prior to and shortly following birth. This work is supported by years of neurological research, which Anna's House continues to pursue. As parents partner with Anna's House to guide their children through the process, lives have dramatically and phenomenally transformed.

www.AnnasHouseLLC.com